BLACK MAGIC

BLACK MAGIC

America's Spyplanes: SR-71 and U-2

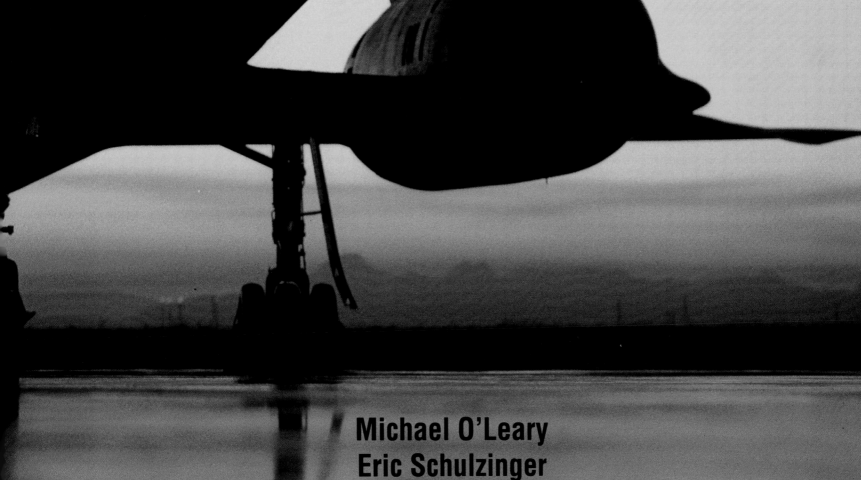

Michael O'Leary
Eric Schulzinger

Motorbooks International
Publishers & Wholesalers ®

First published in 1989 by Motorbooks International
Publishers & Wholesalers Inc, P O Box 2, 729 Prospect
Avenue, Osceola, WI 54020 USA

Printed in Hong Kong

The information in this book is true and complete to the best
of our knowledge. All recommendations are made without
any guarantee on the part of the author or publisher, who
also disclaim any liability incurred in connection with the use
of this data or specific details

We recognize that some words, model names and
designations, for example, mentioned herein are the property
of the trademark holder. We use them for identification
purposes only. This is not an official publication

Library of Congress Cataloging-in-Publication Data
O'Leary, Michael (Michael D.)
    Black magic/Michael O'Leary, Eric Martin Schulzinger.
        p. cm.
    ISBN 0-87938-358-5
    1. Reconnaissance aircraft—United States.
I. Schulzinger, Eric Martin. II. Title.
    UG1242.R40435 1989   89-9245
    358.4'5'0973—dc20   CIP

On the front cover: The SR-71 Blackbird—a sleek black
embodiment of the top secret intrigue of modern hi-tech
espionage.

On the back cover: Portable air conditioning unit in hand,
this SR-71 pilot is suited up and ready to fly. The bulky Dave
Clarke Company pressure suits keep the pilots and RSOs
alive at the near outerspace altitudes where the Blackbirds fly.

In order to obtain the photographs used here several
different types of cameras and film were employed.
Cameras included Nikon F3HP and FM2 bodies equipped
with Nikkor lenses ranging from 18 mm to 180 mm. Leica
R-4 cameras and lenses were utilized along with
Hasselblad cameras and lenses and Mamiya RB-67
cameras and lenses.

Film stocks included Kodachrome 25 and 64, Kodak
VR200 and VR400, Kodacolor 400, Vericolor 160 and
Fujichrome 50. Film sizes included 35 mm and 120 mm.

In order to obtain the aerial photographs, a variety of
aircraft were used including a Learjet, Boeing KC-135Q,
Beech Queen Air and Bonanza, North American B-25
Mitchell and Northrop T-38A Talon.

Few pilots have experienced the thrill of flying an aircraft on its first flight. I've had that thrill twenty times during my sixty-one years in aviation. Twelve of those flights were for my boss, Kelly Johnson.

During early January 1955, Kelly Johnson called me to his office. I'd been testing his latest creation, the XF-104 Starfighter—the first Mach 2 fighter. I had made the first flight in the bird only a year earlier and had worked out most of the bugs. I was now, unofficially, the world's fastest pilot, having been the first to exceed 1000 mph in an aircraft powered by a turbojet.

I was rather pleased with the progress we'd made up to this point—having checked out the USAF's first pilot to fly the Starfighter, Major Chuck Yeager. He was a natural to fly this fantastic new fighter, having been the first pilot to exceed the speed of sound back in 1947.

I reached Kelly's office and took a deep breath before entering. It wasn't often that Kelly called me for a meeting, as we usually met on a daily basis when testing one of his new designs. I paused for a moment, then entered. Kelly was sitting behind his desk and looked up as I said, "Kelly, what can I do for you?"

In his typical style, with only a trace of a smile, he said, "Close the door." I thought this odd and racked my memory for something I could have done that would have displeased him. I knew I hadn't done anything lately, and the only time he had ever chewed me out was back in 1944 when I scared the hell out of him and an Air Force General when I put on a hair-raising demo flight with our new XP–80A Shooting Star. The General was so frightened, he yelled, "Stop him or he'll kill himself!"

Kelly asked, "Tony, do you want to fly a new airplane?"

I asked, "What's it like?"

"Can't tell you," said Kelly. "If you say yes, I will. If you say no, get the hell out of my office."

Being the ultimate advocate of security, Kelly wouldn't tell God if he did not have a reason to know.

"Sure I want to fly your new aircraft!" I said boldly.

After that, Kelly's next statement was, "I want you to keep your lips buttoned about what I'm going to show you. Say nothing to anyone until I tell you who is on this new program. It's Top Secret. You got that?"

I agreed to zip my lips.

Kelly whipped out a roll of plans and spread them over his desk, starting to explain in detail what this new aircraft was all about. The design had a fuselage about the same as the F-104 and the same cockpit and canopy. I was delighted with these facts, since I had helped design certain features on the 104. But the wing, that was something else again. The F-104 had a wing span of about twenty-two feet—probably the shortest ever for a fighter.

"Kelly," I said, "you just had me flying an aircraft with hardly any wing, and now you've got one so long you'll be hard-pressed to see the wingtips from the cockpit."

Kelly finally had a genuine chuckle and got down to explaining what this new program was all about. I liked what I saw and knew immediately that my life would have to be completely changed to cope with the absolute top secret nature of this extraordinary aircraft program.

With the preliminaries out of the way, Kelly gave me the first order of business. "Tony, I want you to work with Dorsey Kammerer [Kelly's favorite crew chief since the early days of the P–38 back in 1937]. I want you both to take the company Beech Bonanza and search for a remote place somewhere in the southwest portion of the United States. I presume this base will hopefully be in southern California, Nevada or Arizona. I want the base to be as remote as possible and yet not completely impossible to get to."

I knew exactly what he had in mind. The dry lakes of the southwest are famous for their super-hard, flat surfaces. We had many years of experience testing new fighters off of Rogers Dry Lake, commonly called Muroc, and now known as Edwards AFB.

I had saved many new fighters on such dry lakes from possible crashes or from not being able to find an airport with adequately long runways for emergencies.

On leaving, Kelly made one more request: "I want you both to change your names, wipe out anything that might connect you with Lockheed, dress in hunting clothes, take supplies to last for two weeks. Now get going, time's wasting!" Kelly added, "One last thing, if anyone starts getting too interested, tell 'em you're going on a special trip to Mexico."

Dorsey and I did find the perfect spot, and, in August 1955, I flew the fantastic new U–2 (though

the design had changed considerably) on its maiden flight. I flew many of the subsequent development test flights to prove the design's worth.

Thirty-four years have passed and this extraordinary aircraft has gone on to perform a service for the good of all mankind. Top officials from NATO countries have often expressed that if it had not been for Kelly Johnson, the Skunk Works and the U-2, the Allies and Soviets would probably have entered World War III.

It is with enormous pride that I recommend this outstanding book on one of the world's greatest aircraft and the follow-up developments from the Skunk Works. These aircraft were created to help preserve, or try to preserve, what's left of what should be a peaceful world.

God bless Lockheed, Kelly Johnson and the U-2!

Tony LeVier
Burbank, California

If your spine is stiffening bamboo, your skin like fabric and you seem to be held together with softly humming flying wires then you may also be one of the early aviators—the ancient pelicans as we have come to be known. The identity is vaguely disturbing. Wasn't it just yesterday that we slipped on helmet and goggles and climbed into biplanes constructed of the same materials which have somehow transformed us, which have since become almost a tangible part of us?

We who have seen and flown what may be the very best of flying times, we who lay claim to the Jennys, Stearmans, Wacos, Travelaires, Swallows, tri-motored Fords, Stinsons and Fleets have come to resemble those birds in various stages of their delapidation. As for the World War II types, we knew and flew a whole grab-bag of military hardware propelled by ear-bashing round engines. Our spirits were unquenchable. Survival ruled the roost and we found countless ways to assure it. Almost.

There has been entirely too much romanticizing about historic airplanes, written by sincere people who obviously never flew them or whose memories are so sweetened by time they have forgotten how uncomfortable, inefficient, cantankerous and sluggish those old airplanes were. And there were very few exceptions. Fly one today and you will be momentarily enchanted—then very soon disillusioned.

When the U-2 and the SR-71 came out of Kelly Johnson's Skunk Works, the aviation development patterns we pelicans had watched with increasing dismay went into full afterburner. The exotic was here and some of us thought the SR-71 was not truly an airplane, but a guided missile—with two men riding piggy-back.

The U-2 achieved flight altitudes we had only dreamed about, even though it flew very much like the old wood, fabric and wire aircraft. Indeed, the U-2's flight characteristics at the lower altitudes and in the pattern resemble nothing more than the cumbersome tri-motored Ford's. And there is not very much difference in "feel" or landing technique. There, once that fact is accepted (and mastered), any comparison ceases. The U-2 climbs to operational altitude with such verve and determination this pelican received a total re-charge of his red corpuscles on every ascension. And cruising along the fences of space became the activation of a dream long standing. Here was the essence and the ultimate flight all in one big-winged bird.

New variants of the U-2 are being built and will serve our reconnaissance people a long time.

Now that it seems almost certain the SR-71s will be permanently retired, we must thank the authors for celebrating in photographic portraits the heyday of such a historic intelligence-gathering machine. Meanwhile, for the next few years at least, count on the U-2R/TR-1 to be our primary spy on world affairs.

Ernest K. Gann
Friday Harbor, Washington

Contents

Acknowledgments

In order to complete a book of this magnitude, we required the goodwill of many people. We would like to give special credit to Ben Rich, Fred Carmody, Richard Stadler, Ernest K. Gann and Tony LeVier for their help and encouragement.

Thanks are also due to Bill Brown, Chuck Guizzo, Gary Hultquist, Andy Stumpf, Brent Thompson, Rich Waide, Norb Budzinski, Tony Chiappetta, Ron Williams, Jerry Hoyt, John Arvesen, Jeff Kertes, Bruce Guberman, Edwin Schnepf, the officers and men of Beale AFB, and the personnel of NASA's High Altitude Missions Branch at Moffett Field.

Special assistance came from Lynn, Jeri, David and Matthew who, in their own way, all made this project possible.

Preface

Few aspects of military aviation are more exciting than the dark, high flying world of intelligence gathering. Most operations are cloaked in deep secrecy and the aircraft tend to be exotic and elusive.

There are many types of intelligence gathering aircraft but for this book we decided to narrow our scope to the specialized aircraft produced by Lockheed: the U-2 series, the TR-1 and the mighty SR-71. In the 1980s, mass journalism developed several new buzz words and terms including "stealth," "black budget" and "covert operations." In reality, all these terms apply over the last three decades as the Advanced Development Projects group created and built aircraft that helped the American government and its Allies gather vital information on expanding Soviet activities.

It is quite amazing to think that the Lockheed U-2 flew for the first time over thirty years ago. Yet, "U-2" remains a household term, and even though the last "short wing" U-2 was retired from NASA service this year, the basic concept remains alive and well in the TR-1 series of aircraft.

As a teenager, my first encounter with the U-2 came about in a strange way. Central Intelligence Agency U-2s were flown into my home airport of Van Nuys, California, where, at the time, Lockheed maintained a fairly large facility. These all-black aircraft, often carrying spurious civilian registrations on the vertical tail came to Van Nuys for modification and overhaul. It is difficult to imagine the reasoning of bringing top-secret CIA U-2s right into the heart of general aviation's busiest airport, but I was not concerned about reasoning at the time, for the all black shapes made fascinating viewing—and excellent subjects for my new Agfa camera. Watching the U-2s depart the Van Nuys airspace was always thrilling, the aircraft's engine roaring and spewing smoke, the U-2 seemed to stand on its tail during takeoff and disappear into the wide California skies.

After college and employment as an aviation journalist, my path would often cross with the U-2 and later Lockheed products in many parts of the world under many different conditions. I guess my fascination with the type remains until this day, for Lockheed's intelligence gatherers are some of the most attractive aircraft ever to grace the airspace.

The creation of this book came about in late 1988 when I was having a discussion with my friend Eric Schulzinger. Both of us were bemoaning the fact that although there were several books available on Lockheed's intelligence gatherers, none really took a close look at the artistic shapes created by the Skunk Works. These aircraft are almost aerial works of art, their shapes enticing and unusual. They deserved to be presented in a format that highlighted the forms of some of the most creative aircraft built.

Eric was responsible for the majority of this creative photography, spending countless hours setting up difficult shots, waiting for just the right lighting and conditions to produce the beautiful photographs that define what *Black Magic* is all about.

My part consisted of gathering the words and supplying a few of the more pedestrian photographs. It was an intense experience and we had the pleasure of meeting many people involved in all types of operations with the Lockheed products. What struck me was the dedication and affection the pilots and crews expressed toward the aircraft they maintained and flew. The aircraft on these pages certainly hold their operators in the grip of their own special magic.

The content and opinion of this book are strictly the author's viewpoint. It does not reflect any viewpoint of Lockheed, the Central Intelligence Agency, or the United States Air Force, although I thank all of them for their unstinting help in making this book a reality.

Michael O'Leary
Los Angeles, California

Chapter one

The base

L ocated in gently rolling foothills bordering the massive Sierra Nevada Mountains, Beale Air Force Base (AFB) is home to some of this country's most advanced, and most classified, aircraft. The base is dominated by a huge monolithic structure that would not be out of place in a futuristic science fiction film. The structure is the ten-story-tall PAVE PAWS sea-launched ballistic missile detection and warning system. Designed to give a vital few minutes of warning against a possible Soviet missile submarine strike against the west coast of America, the imposing structure is operated by the 7th Missile Warning Squadron (part of the Air Force Space Command) and sets the tone for the many unusual and important activities at Beale AFB.

The United States Air Force (USAF) has had a proud tradition of naming its bases after the heroes of American flight, but Beale is an exception. The base gets its name from General Edward F. Beale who, curiously, served both in the Navy and the Army but whose main claim to fame was as founder of the Army's Camel Corps (while also being the largest landholder in California).

A graduate of Annapolis, Beale was assigned to duty under Commodore Stockton in California at the start of the Mexican War. Naval operations were not all that common in California and Beale saw that his future was in other directions. Resigning his Navy commission, Beale became Superintendent of Indian Affairs. Later made an Army brigadier general, Beale was assigned the task of ending the Indian wars that were still plaguing the rapidly expanding state.

California is a state whose geography includes everything from dense forests to extremely high

The Strategic Air Command takes its security seriously—very seriously. Many SAC bases handle nuclear weapons, so the security has to be first-rate. Beale does not house nuclear weapons but the SR-71s, TR-1s and U-2Rs are of such a sensitive nature that vigilance is always required.

mountains to some of the deadliest deserts on the face of the earth. In order to move his troops through these widely differing areas with some degree of efficiency, Beale decided to begin the Army's Camel Corps. The humped beasts were imported to the state and seemed to flourish, although the same can't be said of the cavalry troops who had to become accustomed to the rolling gait of the camel and the creature's decidedly nasty temperament.

The Camel Corps actually achieved some degree of success and Secretary of War Jefferson Davis was rather pleased with the concept. When Davis resigned, however, the Camel Corps fell into disfavor with the new administration and an angry Beale took the camels to his private ranch in southern California where they became his personal pets.

Beale was also Surveyor General of California and Nevada, and accumulated huge land holdings during his term in office—often quickly foreclosing on ranchers who were behind in mortgage payments and acquiring their land for himself at a fraction of its original cost.

These rather draconian methods of land acquisition caught the attention of President Abraham Lincoln who stated, "Well, I appointed him Surveyor General out there and I understand that he is monarch of all he has surveyed."

Beale embodied the attributes of a pioneer of the West—daring and headstrong, he carved his own history. In a way, it is rather fitting that the base is named after a son of the Old West. But what of the base itself? How did it develop into America's main center for manned strategic reconnaissance?

When America entered World War II on 7 December 1941, the nation was basically unprepared for a global conflict, and training facilities were rapidly erected by the hundreds. One such facility opened in October 1942: the Army's Camp Beale, spread out on an amazing 86,000 acres of pastoral California gold rush land. The 13th Armored Division was the first unit into Beale, its tanks churning up the land as they practiced and trained for the deadly battles being waged between the Allies and the Axis. Many other units passed through Beale, and the facility also housed a prisoner of war (POW) camp for captured Axis soldiers. Part of the

Members of the 9th Security Police Squadron stand by as an all-black TR-1B (the second of two examples delivered) dual-control trainer is prepared for a mission (an earlier photograph of this aircraft in an all-white training scheme appears elsewhere in this book). The 9th Security Police Squadron performs a dual function by providing protection for Beale's critical national defense assets as well as providing the base residents with professional police services.

WARNING

Restricted Area

It is unlawful to enter this area without permission of the Installation Commander.
Sec. 21, Internal Security Act of 1950;50 U.S.C. 797

While on this Installation all personnel and the property under their control are subject to search.

Use of deadly force authorized.

This area is patrolled by military working dog teams.

During the early 1980s, several SAC missile silos and a B-52 facility were attacked and damaged by anti-nuclear vandals. The resulting publicity made SAC tighten security even more, and the statement "use of deadly force authorized" was not to be taken lightly.

facility was made into a large hospital and, at the end of the war, the camp served as a very welcome West Coast separation center.

In 1947, the base was declared surplus and the facility, which once housed up to 60,000 personnel, became almost as much of a ghost town as some of the historic small gold mining camps dotting the nearby Sierras.

During the late 1940s, the United States Air Force became a separate service, and the Soviet Union turned from an ally into a very real and dangerous threat to the Western powers. During this period, the mighty Strategic Air Command (SAC) come into existence, led by the iconoclastic, cigar-chomping General Curtis LeMay. LeMay immediately set out to make SAC the most powerful and influential of all USAF commands; the construction of huge bases across the world was begun to accommodate SAC's rapidly increasing force of heavy bombers.

In 1948, Beale was acquired by the USAF and was used for bombardier/navigator training for about three years. The base received a number of assignments until being put under the wing of SAC in 1956. SAC immediately began to reconstruct the base to its own specifications, which included the construction of a typically huge SAC runway. The base went into operation on 27 August 1958, with a runway 12,000 feet long and 500 feet wide.

Initially housing KC-135 Stratotankers, Beale also became a support base for the new Titan Intercontinental Ballistic Missiles. With the phase-out of the Titan I program in 1965, Beale took on the new role of aerial intelligence gathering—one which the base has been associated with ever since.

In 1965, the 4200th Strategic Reconnaissance Wing (SRW) was activated with the stunning new Lockheed SR-71 Blackbird, an aircraft that had been revealed to the American public a short time previously by President Lyndon Johnson. Capable of sustained flights over Mach 3, the Lockheed-built aircraft had been heavily shrouded in secrecy during its development and flight test program. Beale, fairly remote from prying eyes, was an excellent headquarters for the ultimate SAC reconnaissance aircraft.

Redesignated the 9th Strategic Reconnaissance Wing just one and a half years later, the reconnaissance community began to completely take over the base when the 17th Bombardment Wing departed with its mighty Boeing B-52s. It was replaced by the 100th Air Refueling Wing flying KC-135s and dedicated to feeding the hungry Blackbirds.

In a consolidation of resources, the 9th SRW absorbed the Lockheed U-2s of the 99th Strategic Reconnaissance Squadron (SRS), thus making Beale the major American strategic reconnaissance base.

With these unique aviation activities in one place, it was natural that Beale became home for the massive PAVE PAWS phased-array radar.

Residents in the nearby towns of Marysville and Yuba City quickly became accustomed to the noise from the booming Blackbird afterburners as the exotic craft staged out of Beale for their long-distance missions. They also became accustomed to the near silent flight of the U-2s and later U-2Rs as they wheeled overhead in the clear California sky, not unlike huge hawks riding out the thermals generated by the rolling hills.

Over the years, Beale has been the starting point for many classified missions essential to the security of the nation. These missions will undoubtedly remain classified for many years to come— both because of the concerns of the government of the United States and of the Allies from whose bases these intelligence gathering aircraft have operated.

As we approach the end of 1989, the future of reconnaissance activities at Beale AFB is open to some speculation. The stunning cost of SR-71 operations (reported by some sources to be as high as $250,000 per flight hour) has led the more budget-minded politicians to call for added reliance on reconnaissance satellites and to consign the proud SR fleet to mothballs. It has also been rumored that a USAF training wing will be assigned to Beale. Whatever the outcome, modern history has been written at this base.

The Beale AFB control tower looms behind one of Beale's signs. From the tower, missions are launched to all parts of the globe.

9th Security Police Squadron makes a regular sweep of the Beale ramp. With all of Beale's acreage, regular motorized patrols are undertaken to ensure perimeter security.

*Vital elements of the overall Beale mission, the
Stratotankers are specially configured to cater to the
Blackbird's specialized needs while the sleek all-white
Talons are used to monitor each SR-71 mission and to
provide a variety of training flights for 9th SRW pilots.*

Chapter two

Blackbirds

History was made in several ways on 29 February 1964, when President Lyndon B. Johnson revealed that America was flying a new, highly advanced aircraft—an aircraft that was so different in appearance from anything else in the sky that the new plane might as well have come from outer space. Johnson used photographs of a Lockheed YF-12A to back up his statements. It was a moment to relish, the press had been caught flat-footed and American aeronautical prestige had taken a giant leap forward.

Just a few short months later (on 24 July), Johnson made yet another amazing announcement. The President revealed that Lockheed had developed a new plane called the SR-71, an aircraft dedicated to strategic reconnaissance with performance so advanced that no other aircraft (Allied or Soviet) could catch it. Johnson made a slight error in his speech, referring to the new design as the "SR-71" rather than by the new plane's correct designation of "RS-71." No one likes to correct a President, and the new design became for all-time the SR-71.

How had such a family of advanced aircraft come into being under such a veil of secrecy? The Central Intelligence Agency, in its ever growing need to monitor Soviet activities, felt that the highly-successful Lockheed U-2 would quickly become vulnerable to growing Soviet defenses. Impressed by the efficiency of Lockheed, Kelly Johnson and the "Skunk Works," then-CIA director Richard Bissell wondered out loud if a more advanced reconnais-

With its sleek high-tech looks, it's difficult to believe that the basic SR-71 is approaching three decades in age. Still holding many speed and altitude records, the SR-71 remains a shining example of superior American aeronautical design. These three SR-71s of the 1st SRS of the 9th are seen on the ramp at Beale, the morning sun glinting off their flat black flanks. The middle aircraft is the SR-71B, a two-seat dual-control trainer used to teach transitioning USAF pilots the fine art of operating the Blackbird.

sance aircraft could be built and flown, an aircraft that would not need to worry about Soviet defenses for some time to come. To Johnson and his team this was an open challenge and the floodgates of aeronautical creativity were opened wide.

During 1956, the team went to work on several different ideas. Some consideration was given to modifying the U-2 to see if more performance could be obtained from the basic design. "We made many studies and tests to improve the survivability of the U-2 by attempting to fly higher and faster as well as reducing its radar cross-section and providing both infrared and radar jamming gear," stated Kelly Johnson. However, the only real gain that could be made with the design was an increase in cruise altitude so further effort in that direction was abandoned.

During this time period, there was a great deal of speculation that jet fuel would be replaced by other fuels including liquid hydrogen and boron slurries. Much money and time were expended by several companies in studying these different modes of propulsion. Even though these fuels promised aircraft that could cruise at over 100,000 ft, the idea was eventually scrapped because of the difficulty in producing the fuel and ensuring that it could be available to aircraft operating from a wide variety of locations, some of them primitive and in foreign countries.

Johnson and his team came up with a set of guidelines for the new aircraft: It must be relatively easy to operate and prepare for a mission, it would have to fly at speeds above Mach 3 for lengthy periods of times, and it would have to have a design cruise altitude of over 80,000 ft. In order to delay detection by the Soviets, the new aircraft would also have to have the lowest radar cross-section possible while electronic countermeasures (ECM) would be carried to negate other threats. Two engines would also be required for safety of operations.

When an aircraft is propelled at increasing speed through the atmosphere, its skin begins to heat up from the advancing flow of molecules around the airframe. Most aircraft are built of aluminum alloys but the hotter aluminum gets, the more the soft metal loses its overall strength. Thus, the new aircraft would be built of newly developed titanium and stainless steel alloys. Many other new materials would have to be developed that could stand the stress of high speed and high altitude. New plastics needed to be formulated along with new fluids and electrical wiring. Even items such as wheels and tires had to be carefully thought out because of the extended time the new design would spend at high speeds, allowing the entire airframe to "heat soak."

Other companies were also working on advanced aircraft and Kelly and his team would study data on these new designs whenever they could get their hands on them to see what else the CIA and USAF were considering. "We were evaluated against some very interesting designs by General Dynamics and a Navy design," recalled Johnson. "This latter concept was proposed as a ramjet-powered rubber inflatable machine, initially carried to altitude by a balloon and then rocket boosted to a speed where the ramjets could produce thrust. Our studies on this aircraft proved it to be totally unfeasible. The carrying balloon had to be a mile in diameter to lift the unit, which had a proposed wing area of 1/7th of an acre!"

General Dynamics' Convair division proposed using a ramjet-powered Mach 4 aircraft carried by a B-58 Hustler bomber and dropped when the desired speed and altitude were achieved. With the new design in place under its belly, the Hustler could not achieve the required speed to launch the ramjet craft.

With the small design team working overtime, the design progressed and problems were met and defeated one by one. The USAF was deeply interested in the work being carried out by the Advanced Development Projects (ADP) group (otherwise known as the Skunk Works) and felt that the new plane could be operated as a very potent interceptor to be utilized against possible new generations of Soviet manned bombers. Funding for the new designs was kept very "black" and not open to government scrutiny. Much of the funding was supplied to Lockheed through various CIA accounts, not unlike the manner in which the U-2 was funded.

On 29 August 1959, the A-12 (a Lockheed designation) was picked as the winner (there was little doubt) over the other projects. The CIA issued a contract to test scale models of the new design and to build a full-scale mock-up. Complete approval for the program came on 30 January 1960, to finish designing, manufacturing and testing on twelve new aircraft.

Johnson, assisted by the talented Ben Rich, managed to overcome problems that other companies could not. Lockheed had been working with titanium since 1949. A difficult metal at the best of times, much study was expended on how to work with it and make it useful for aircraft manufacturing. "We attempted to attain high strength-weight ratios, good ductility, and relatively cheap structures, which did not develop very rapidly," Johnson recalled.

Lots of other improvisations had to be undertaken to create the new aircraft for the CIA. "There were no control cables which would take the required number of cycles safely," said Johnson. "We had to have special ones made of Elgiloy, the material used for watch springs."

Specially tempered glass protects the SR-71 pilot from the effects of very high speed flight. At Mach 3 plus, the entire airframe begins to heat up as the aircraft roars along on its assigned mission. The heat, combined with the near lack of atmospheric pressure at operational altitudes, and the threat of various cosmic rays, makes for a very hostile environment from which the two crewmembers must be protected.

Because of the geographical location of Beale AFB, the facility is quite often subjected to thick, mysterious ground fogs, especially during the winter months. An SR-71 is seen here in its hangar, shrouded in mist as it awaits the next mission.

Equipment for the interior of the aircraft had to be carefully tested and often remanufactured to meet the team's very particular needs. "In the field of equipment there was an amazing lack of high temperature electronic gear, particularly in the areas of wires, plugs, transducers and so on. Many vendors told us they had transducers good for 1,000 degrees F. operating temperatures, but when we tested the gear we found it had mainly been designed for rocket testing and its life span was very short. Due essentially to temperature lag, the inside of the unit seldom got hot. There were no hydraulic fluids or pumps that could take operating temperatures continuously of approximately 600 degrees F. There were no hydraulic seals suitable for such an environment," stated Johnson.

advanced features of the A-12 could not be fully tested until the J58s were ready and installed during the first part of 1963. From that point on, the A-12 was a whole new airplane.

Problems with heat soon cropped up. Ben Rich had devised a red and white paint for the national insignia (even though the A-12 was a CIA aircraft, it apparently was USAF funded and at least one example carried USAF insignia and national markings) that hopefully would withstand high speeds. It didn't. Some of the plastic areas gave trouble while other areas also showed related developmental problems. As with other ADP aircraft, problems were attacked and beaten one by one.

The world press was shocked at President Johnson's 29 February 1964 statement about the aircraft—even the aviation press was taken aback, secrecy had been that good. Although President Johnson had never really gotten down to stating exactly what the new plane's role was or who was operating the aircraft, he did make a few other confusing statements. It is not known if Johnson's statements were a slip of the lip or deliberate misinformation, but he referred to the A-12 as the A-11 and then used photos of the YF-12A to illustrate the aircraft. Presidential blunderings aside, it had to be a proud moment for Kelly Johnson, Ben Rich and the whole ADP team when their creation was revealed to the world.

With its sleekly long fuselage, huge twin engines and double delta wing, there was little doubt that the A-12 was one hot machine. A single-seater, CIA-operated A-12s covered the world, several of the twelve examples being lost in training and operational accidents. One modified A-12 carrying a D-21 ramjet reconnaissance drone was destroyed during the first test separation of aircraft and drone, resulting in one fatality.

A-12 operations remain sealed in CIA archives (not to be made public until the next century) but the surviving examples (the type was withdrawn from operations in 1968 for unknown reasons) can be seen in open storage at Palmdale's Plant 42, where they have been for many years.

As mentioned earlier, the USAF had great interest in the design as an interceptor to meet and destroy a new generation of Soviet manned bombers (a new generation which, by the way, did not materialize until two decades later). There has

This wide-angle view emphasizes the strange, other-worldly appearance of the SR-71. Every inch of the airframe was designed for optimum performance in the most hostile of environments: the near outer space atmosphere in which the intelligence gathering Blackbird operates.

been considerable speculation that the A-12 was the fastest of all three aircraft to come out of the basic design (A-12, YF-12, SR-71) with a top speed around Mach 3.6 at 92,000 ft, but these performance figures for all three aircraft remain classified, so this cannot be verified.

The YF-12 was to carry the advanced Hughes ASG-18/GAR-19 fire control and missile system and have a two-man crew. To increase stability, a large folding fin was added under the rear fuselage (folding flat during takeoff and landing), and missile bays in the fuselage to carry the three advanced AIM-47A weapons.

Also assembled at Groom Lake and prepared for flight, the first USAF YF-12 flew on 7 August 1963 with James Eastham at the controls. Only three YF-12s were built, some parties considered the aircraft a "cover-up" for the SR-71 program. It does not appear that the YF-12 was used for anything *but* the development of a successful interceptor.

The program had many hurdles to overcome including the launching of a missile from an aircraft already traveling Mach 3. Kelly Johnson wrote, "Great difficulty existed in obtaining instrumentation satisfactory for measuring pressures and air velocity over the speed altitude spectrum. This is particularly true of conditions in the engine inlet and ejector. This necessitated the development of water-cooled instrumentation packages, which were quite clumsy, but did provide a means for making the millions of pressure measurements required through the development tests.

"I would say the the greatest problem encountered in-flight had to do with the transonic speed region, where it was extremely difficult to correlate the results from wind tunnel tests and flight tests.

"The next greatest problem had to do with the development of the air inlet control system, which involved scheduling the air inlet spike position, and various by-pass door arrangements, to maintain the optimum shock position on the cowl, and minimum drag. Operating forces as high as fourteen tons can develop on the spike. This requires massive hydraulic power and extremely fast sensing of the various design parameters to restart the inlet.

"The aircraft showed itself to have excellent flight characteristics throughout its speed range, particularly on takeoff and landing. Visibility was good, but the pilots initially complained of a very high glare flying at high altitudes. The use of non-reflective coatings on instruments, and other areas, definitely helped this condition."

Hughes had developed an excellent weapon system (forerunner of today's efficient and combat-proven Phoenix) in the pulse-Doppler ASG-18 radar unit and GAR-9 (later redesignated AIM-74A) long-

Blackbird details. SR-71s quite often carry very temporary artwork on their vertical tail surfaces. Usually applied with chalk, these sometimes whimsical touches are usually the brainstorm of the crew chief and provide a needed touch of humor in what is otherwise a very serious mission.

range missile. These systems had originally been developed for the North American F-108 Rapier, an advanced stainless-steel interceptor, but when that program had been canceled because of technical delays and cost overruns, the radar and missile were transferred to the Lockheed project.

The second cockpit in the YF-12 was occupied by the Fire Control Officer (FCO) who operated the radar to acquire, track and fire at hostile targets. Because of the high speed of the YF-12, a missile launch could travel up to 150 miles and the tracking system was sophisticated enough to track and destroy supersonic targets at altitudes between sea level and 100,000 ft. After three years of testing and fine tuning, the system was enjoying an excellent ninety percent success rate against drone targets.

Lockheed wanted to build a definitive F-12B interceptor but the Kennedy Administration's new Secretary of Defense, Robert Sylvester McNamara, had other ideas. McNamara was a politician who firmly believed that the day of the manned combat aircraft was pretty much over. If manned aircraft had to be built, they should be designed to serve several armed services in a variety of different ways. Hence was born McNamara's pet aircraft, the F-111. Even though Congress had voted a large budget for the development of the F-12B, McNamara managed to get the project canceled and allocated the funds towards his own projects. Kelly Johnson and his team were extremely disappointed.

Two of the YF-12s were passed on to NASA where they performed sterling service in the area of high-speed research for commercial transports. The third YF-12 was extensively modified to create the dual-control SR-71C which was, rather appropriately, given the name *The Bastard.*

Although the A-12 remains shrouded in secrecy and the YF-12 was stopped short by politicians, the final family member of the basic design conceived in the late 1950s was to make Lockheed world famous.

In January 1961, Kelly Johnson made his first proposal for an advanced strategic reconnaissance aircraft to Dr. Joseph Charyk (then Secretary of the Air Force), Colonel Leo Gary (project officer on the YF-12) and Lew Meyer (USAF financial officer). The meeting was favorable to all concerned and ADP began to make initial studies into what would become the SR-71. Opposition in the USAF came from those siding with the North American XB-70 program which had run into some problems as a bomber and was now being considered as a strategic reconnaissance platform.

An SR-71 mockup was built and the USAF liked what they saw. Johnson continued discussions with General Curtis LeMay of the Strategic Air Command and, on 28 December 1962, a contract was issued to Lockheed for the production of the first batch of six SR-71s.

Johnson recalled the basic design features of the SR-71 along with the aircraft's mission requirements, "Having chosen the required performance in speed, altitude and range, it was immediately evident that a thin delta-wing planform was required with a very moderate wing loading to allow flight at very high altitude. A long, slender fuselage was necessary to contain most of the fuel as well as the landing gear and payloads. To reduce the wing trim drag, the fuselage was fitted with lateral surfaces called chines, which actually converted the forward fuselage into a fixed canard which developed lift.

"The hardest design problem on the airplane was making the engine air inlet and ejector work properly. The inlet cone moves almost three feet to keep the shock wave where we want it. A hydraulic actuator, computer controlled, has to provide operating forces of up to 31,000 pounds under certain flow conditions in the nacelles. To account for the effect of the fuselage chine airflow, the inlets are pointed down and in toward the fuselage.

"The use of dual vertical tails canted inward on the engine nacelles took advantage of the chine vortex in such a way that the directional stability improves as the angle of attack of the aircraft increases."

To the casual observer, the A-12, YF-12 and SR-71 look like the same aircraft. Yet, there are many important differences between them—both in mission and design. For example, the gross weight of the SR-71 is about 172,000 pounds, compared to the 120,000 pound gross weight of the A-12. The SR-71 is longer and has broader chines while the second cockpit houses the Reconnaissance Systems Officer (RSO).

As mentioned earlier, various aerodynamic improvements have been incorporated into the SR-71, especially the air intake systems.

Enjoying the benefits of research and flight test programs undertaken on the A-12 and YF-12, the first SR-71A flew on 22 December 1964 with pilot Robert J. Gilliland. The first flight took place at the much more public (compared to Groom Lake) Plant 42 in Palmdale, California, the sleek new plane being hotly pursued by a trio of F-104 Starfighter chase planes. The production run of SR-71s would eventually comprise a total of thirty-two aircraft.

The majority of the SR-71 flight test program took place at nearby Edwards AFB where the first three aircraft were used extensively. This was mainly a USAF program, the CIA pretty much having pulled out during the first part of the 1960s.

Several SRs (or "Blackbirds" as the type became nicknamed early in its career) were lost during the early days of testing and operational

Close-ups of the Blackbird's titanium structure show the amount of advanced detailed engineering that went into creating an aircraft that would venture where no others could.

WARNING
T CONTAINS A SEAT
EXPLOSIVE
NTEWANCE MANUAL

The unique two-seat SR-71B carries another fully instrumented dual-control cockpit mounted behind and above the normal pilot position. The plane is used exclusively for training and is not capable of strategic reconnaissance missions.

deployment. One aircraft came apart following a pitch-up at altitude when an engine had an unstart (an odd event where the engine's shockwave is interrupted, causing a loss of power, violent yawing and possible airframe failure under the high G loads imposed by the maneuver). Two other aircraft were lost when tires blew out on landing, resulting in the aircraft leaving the runway and being destroyed in fires when the magnesium wheels began to burn. These two accidents resulted in modifications to the tires and wheels.

Today, the surviving SR-71 force is headquartered at Beale Air Force Base. Permanent detachments (Dets) were established in Britain and Okinawa. Det 4 operates out of RAF Mildenhall but Det 1 at Kadena Air Base in Okinawa was phased out of operation as this book was being prepared.

SR-71 missions are not spur of the moment flights. Planning usually starts two days in advance (of course, in times of emergency this time would be cut considerably). Routes are carefully planned and crews thoroughly briefed. SR-71 crews usually stay together for their entire tour of duty since successful operations demand that the two men work closely (and well) together. "You really have to rely on your partner," said one SR backseater at Beale. "You begin to think and act alike. And that's important in order to stay alive."

Suit-ups are not unlike those performed by the base's TR-1 crews. And the suits worn by the crews are even similar. SR-71 crews don the Dave Clark S1030 while the TR-1 pilots wear the S1010B. The suits are bulky and require assistance from the PSD crew to get into and close up. Beale's PSD force employs about 100 people who make sure the pilot and RSO are physically in good shape and that their suits are always in top-notch condition. The failure of a suit at altitude does not bear consideration. Immediately before suit-up, the crew is given a medical check. Suit-up is left to the last so as not to tire the crew before launching on what will be a very demanding mission even for the fittest of pilots (some pilots can lose up to seven pounds per flight).

The PSD van transports the pilots to the aircraft which is contained in its hangar on the Beale flight line. While the crew has been undergoing physical checks and suiting up, the aircraft has been minute-

As the morning mists burn off at Beale, a Blackbird is prepared for its day's work. Maintenance crews perform many checks to ensure the airframe and its associated complex systems are in fully operational condition. Highly skilled specialists of the 9th Strategic Reconnaissance Wing take their job seriously, knowing that anything less than 100 percent effort could imperil a costly mission vital to national security.

While maintenance men and systems technicians prepare the aircraft, nav planners carefully chart the Blackbird's flight plan. Much detail planning goes into each mission, calculating weather conditions, fuel requirements, flight parameters and territory over which the flight will be operating.

In the Physiological Support Division (PSD) facility, the Dave Clark Company S1030 pressure suits await the pilots and reconnaissance systems officers (RSO). These custom-made suits are what keep the crews alive at altitude. Costing $30,000 apiece, the S1030s (known as "Daveys" by the crews) are themselves superb examples of advanced engineering.

ly inspected by another SR crew. The inspecting crew report directly to the flight crew and brief on the condition of the plane and outline any squawks (operational problems or malfunctioning equipment). In reality, a squawk is uncommon. The crew chief and his staff have spent hours inspecting and probing the SR for any possible mechanical problems. "If the check crew and the crew chief say the bird is ready to go, it's ready to go," said an SR-71 driver out of Beale. "They're pros and I give them my full trust."

Clambering up the boarding ramp in the S1030s is a bit difficult and the PSD crew once again offers assistance. Once the pilot and RSO are in the aircraft, the PSD people make sure they are strapped into their various harnesses and double check that the suit is mated with the aircraft's environmental systems. Once the crew's cockpit needs have been provided for, the PSD crew depart the hangar and the SR's crew chief takes over in what is a carefully orchestrated ballet between men and machine.

The interior of each Blackbird "nest" on the Beale flight line is equipped with its own powerful self-start system (lots of power is required to get those big engines running) and the start process of each engine is a rather awesome spectacle. To get the JP-7 fuel going, the pilot has to fire a shot of Triethyl Borane (TEB) into the engine while the rpm is building up to get the whole mess running. At night, this can be spectacular, as the TEB burns with an unearthly green flame before igniting the J58 into action.

Three hours before a mission, the Blackbird crew reports to the PSD for a medical check, a high-protein meal and donning of the Dave Clark suits. Getting into the suits requires the help of two PSD specialists and takes about 20 minutes. The crew then breathes 100 percent oxygen for 30 minutes to eliminate nitrogen from their blood, reducing the possibility of bends.

While the SR-71 pilot and RSO are going through their routines, work on the mission aircraft proceeds. This 9th SRW crewman is preparing to remove the protective red surfaces that cover easily damaged areas of the Blackbird. Note how the aircraft's serial number has been stenciled on each removable item.

Once both engines are successfully running, all power lines are disconnected from the airframe and the pilot gingerly taxis the SR from its nest and out onto the ramp, carefully guided by the crew chief. At this point, the airframe of the SR is still "loose" and JP-7 dribbles and drips from the airframe as the all-black plane gently rocks its way out of the hangar.

Raw fuel dripping from an airplane while its engines are lit is an explosively dangerous situation. But this is a special airplane and it is powered by a very special fuel: JP-7. The volatility of JP-7 is so low that under normal conditions you could drop a lit cigarette into a puddle of the fuel without igniting it. Not until the SR-71's airframe has "heated-up" will the fuel spill stop and it will take some flying before that happens.

At a pre-designated point on the taxiway, the SR has chocks placed under the wheels and an engine run is performed while a final airframe and systems check is undertaken. If everything is "go"

(and it usually is), the chocks are pulled with an affirmative thumbs-up and the Blackbird trundles toward the active.

In the cockpit, the pilot stands on the brakes, brings the engines up to full military power, pops the brakes, lets the Blackbird roll a few feet and then shoves the throttles through the gate into afterburner. The Beale countryside rocks to the white heat explosion that pours forth from the J58s. A beautiful shock wave emerges from the engines, trailing flaming diamonds much like some mythical beast, and the SR lurches forward on a charge down the runway. At twilight, this scene can be particularly magnificent.

All pre-flight maintenance takes place in the Blackbird's alert hangar.

Since a tanker is waiting ahead to refuel the thirsty Blackbird, the takeofff run is not overly lengthy considering the aerodynamic shape of the aircraft. The Blackbird is usually airborne in about 5,000 ft, carefully monitored by one or two T-38s that fly alongside to make sure the USAF's investment is operating as it should be.

The pilot yanks the gear lever as soon as possible in order to not exceed the gear's 300 knot retraction limit. From that point on, it's like riding a Fourth of July rocket as the Blackbird climbs out to meet the waiting KC-135Q. Rate of climb exceeds 10,000 feet per minute (fpm) as the Blackbird heads for the tanker. Joining the tanker takes some skill since the Blackbird's refueling port is located well behind the crew stations. The refueling is carefully monitored since at least one Blackbird was lost when it rammed the tanker aircraft.

After refueling, the Blackbird heads up to about 33,000 ft and then noses over in a slight dive to about 28,000 to pass through the sound barrier. At this point, the stick is brought back and the Blackbird heads for the altitudes at which it was designed to operate.

The SR-71 is guided to its target by an advanced pre-programmed inertial navigation system that is unfailingly reliable. Depending on the distance to and from the chosen target, several refuelings may be necessary. These are very tiring for the crew and the aircraft has to come down from its cruising altitude (thought to be 82–85,000 ft with a mission payload) for the refueling process to begin all over again.

Nearing the target, the show is run by the RSO while the pilot concentrates on "driving" the aircraft. Depending on the mission, a variety of sensors and/or cameras can be carried. With Soviet defenses being as advanced as they are, few missions take the Blackbird into areas of extreme hazard (a published report in March 1989, however, voiced a Soviet claim that a Blackbird had either flown over or come uncomfortably near Soviet airspace near the top of the world).

The Blackbird fleet is particularly valuable for gathering information from places like Nicaragua or Cuba, areas that are defended but basically unable to bring down the aircraft at altitude and speed.

With recently improved relations with the Chinese and Russians, it is vitally important in terms of world politics that the Blackbirds fly on the straight

Before the flight, the SR's fuel system is serviced with liquid nitrogen—presenting a rather strange scene as vapor swirls around aircraft and equipment. Nitrogen pressurizes the fuel system and then helps to purge it of vapor as the fuel supply is depleted.

Blackbird pilots are volunteers and must go through a battery of physical and psychological tests before being accepted for crew training.

and narrow, navigating a precise path just outside these nations' airspace while sensors "look" deep into their territory to gather vital information. Depending on the sensor package carried, the Blackbird can cover about 100,000 square miles of territory per hour.

Over the past decade, the safety factor of flying the Blackbird has dramatically increased. This is primarily due to the fact that the top of the "learning curve" has been reached and that the aircraft can be predictably operated over a known set of parameters with a very definite amount of safety.

However, flying such exotic aircraft as the SR–71 can be a hazardous job. During April 1989, an SR–71A, operating out of Beale AFB, was lost when it crashed into the South China Sea while on a classified mission. Fortunately, both crewmembers had time to safely eject, and they were quickly plucked out of the water by search and rescue (SAR) forces.

On returning from a mission, the Blackbird begins a very gradual descent, usually at about 500 fpm, allowing the airframe to gradually cool down as the speed is reduced. Depending on the mission, another refueling may be required on the way back down. When the nose is raised a bit, drag increases

and the Blackbird can slow dramatically for landing, using its own aerodynamic braking powers. The gear is lowered to help cool tires and wheels before landing, and touchdown at base is usually at about 150 to 155 knots. If the landing looks to be a bit hot, surplus fuel can be rapidly jettisoned.

When watching a Blackbird come in for landing at Beale, the sink rate of the aircraft looks like the proverbial brick but the plane is always under control. During this phase of operation, the pilot gets a good work out since control forces are fairly heavy. On landing, the pilot pulls a handle to pop a large forty-foot-diameter drag chute that helps the sleek Blackbird slow down on the Beale runway.

Once the aircraft is off the active, the plane is carefully guided back to its normal parking area. Once parked in its nest, the ground crew immediately positions cooling fans around the landing gear to help get rid of heat soak along with the heat generated by the use of the brakes. The airframe is still hot and makes audible noises as it cools off in the hangar, contracting back to its original shape (at maximum speed, the SR actually changes its dimensions by about a half-inch due to the forces of excessive heat, a factor that also seals off the fuel tanks at altitude).

After each operation, the ground crew carefully checks out the airframe to make sure no damage has been incurred during the mission. These inspections are very important, especially when the aircraft's advancing age is taken into consideration.

This inspection takes several hours and while this is going on, the crew is going through a thorough debrief while the sensor and/or camera data is removed from the aircraft and closely scrutinized.

Other forms of intelligence gathering have supplemented the work of the SR-71 fleet. Advanced satellites are able to collect information with much less risk but, in many ways, they are not as flexible as the SR-71. Recently, the cost of operating the SR-71 fleet has come under considerable scrutiny. One scource states that to keep nine SR-71s operational with associated crews and tankers is equal in cost to maintaining two tactical fighter wings in Europe.

The effectiveness of the SR-71 fleet in gathering information was recently emphasized by an Air Force official who stated that the SRs had been fired upon over 1,000 times. The distinction was not made between aircraft and missile attacks, but the official went on to say that many of the attacks had happened while SRs were operating over North Korea. The amazing thing about this statement is that not one SR has ever been damaged by enemy action.

Once pilot Major Terry Pappas and RSO Captain John Manzi are fully dressed and their suits checked, they are put in the transport van for the ride to the aircraft. These few minutes of horizontal relaxation help the crew mentally prepare for the difficult mission ahead.

On 6 September 1976, Soviet Lt. Viktor Belenko made an important intelligence gift to the West when he defected with a MiG–25 interceptor. Taking off from the Soviet base at Sikharovka, Belenko flew to Hakodate Airport in Japan, where he made a hard but safe landing. Before the aircraft was eventually returned to the Soviets, American and Allied intelligence experts examined the plane and its systems in minute detail.

Capable of speeds in excess of Mach 3, the MiG–25 had been considered a very realistic threat for the Blackbird fleet. During interrogation, Belenko stated that the MiG–25s had indeed been used for Blackbird intercepts but they could not catch the American high fliers. Belenko said he had been personally involved with some of these attempted

Since the crew is encumbered in their bulky pressure suits, a walk-around inspection of their aircraft is not possible, so the task is performed by their "buddy crew"—the backup crew for the mission. Major Duane Noll gives the crew his report on the aircraft which is "ready to launch." Because of the nature of the operation, pilots and RSOs are usually teamed for their three- or four-year tour on Blackbirds.

The crew is accompanied by two PSD specialists to aid the pilot and RSO in strapping into the parachute and harness systems. At this point, the portable air conditioners (which keep the crew cool during the drive to the aircraft) are disconnected and the suits are plugged into the environmental system of the aircraft.

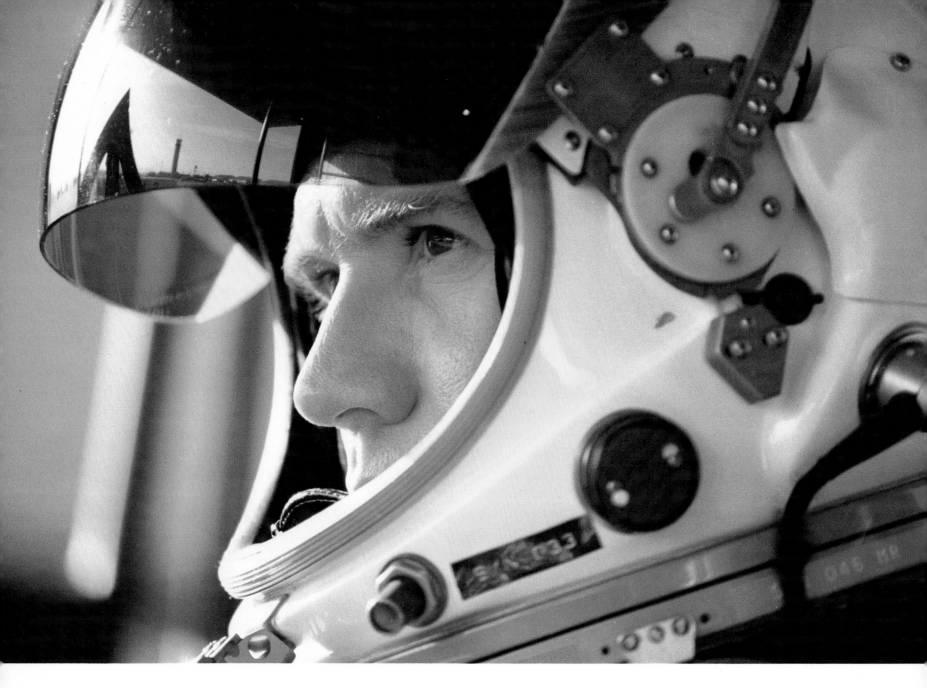

Once in the cockpit, the RSO has just two small side windows for outside visibility. The cockpits are protected with heavy metal frames and tempered glass to withstand the extreme temperatures. At mission altitude and speed, temperatures around the cockpit area can rise to 622 degrees F.

intercepts, but was critical of the MiG–25's time to accelerate to high speeds—one of the prime reasons for intercept failures. Belenko also stated that top Mach numbers were hard to maintain once the fighter was on its "step" and that there were some stability problems at high speeds.

The USAF has pretty much confirmed that the SR-71 program will be completely phased out of operation during October 1989. The USAF plans to move a Cessna T-37 training wing into Beale (although the U-2Rs and TR-1As will presumably continue to use the Beale facility.)

"We've already put in a bid for two of the SRs," said one NASA official who wished to remain un-identified. There is some possibility that a smaller force of SRs will be kept operational. Will the SR-71 disappear from the skies forever at the end of 1989? It's hard to tell when you're dealing with Black Magic!

Lockheed SR-71A specifications

Span	55 ft 6 in
Length	107 ft 4 in
Height	18 ft 6 in
Wing area	1,795 sq ft
Empty weight	67,550 lbs
Maximum weight	172,000 lbs
Maximum speed	1,875 kts (estimated)
Limiting mach number	3.2
Ceiling	88,000 ft (estimated)
Range	3,500 miles (unrefueled)
Sensor payload	3,750 lbs (estimated)
Powerplant	Two Pratt & Whitney J58s of 32,500 lb static thrust each

Settling in for the mission. The pilot, Major Terry Pappas, and RSO Captain John Manzi, relax for a moment while last minute checks are performed before engine start.

The magnificent Pratt & Whitney J58 powerplant is one of the main keys to the SR-71's protracted history of success. The bypass turbojet pumps out a stunning 32,500 pounds of thrust (in afterburner) and both engines consume 8,000 gallons per hour at operational settings. In order to start the J58, an air start system is built into the operational hangars. Since the JP-7 has a very high flash point, tetraethyl borane (TEB) is injected during the start procedure to lower the flash point and produce easier ignition. The TEB gives off a green flame when ignited, which can be seen here.

Slightly advancing the throttles, the Blackbird carefully moves out of the hangar and heads to the active runway while a ground crewman carefully watches for anything abnormal.

The specialized tankers of the 349th and 350th ARS become airborne before the launch of the SR. Two tankers take off for each Blackbird mission. If the lead tanker has to abort, the secondary tanker can immediately take the lead. The KC-135Qs carry the specialized JP-7 fuel required by the SR's J58 powerplants.

Generating a sea of heat waves, the Blackbird launches down the Beale taxiway.

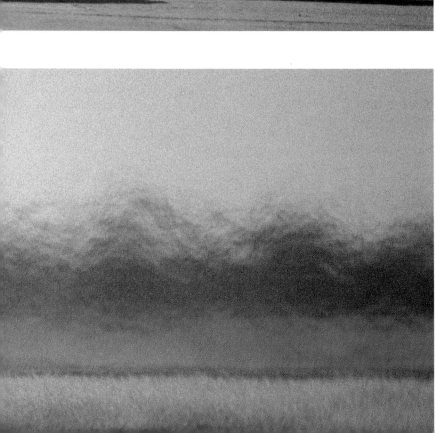

The SR-71's J58 afterburners are ignited with a squirt of TEB since, once again, the JP-7 is particularly difficult to ignite—even when afterburner is selected. The countryside around Beale shakes as the 65,000 pounds of white-hot thrust rips the air asunder.

At twilight, the afterburners of the J58s produce a distinctive diamond shock pattern. In less than 20 seconds, the Blackbird has achieved over 200 knots of forward speed. In order to reduce airframe fatigue and ensure better control if an engine malfunctions, takeoffs are usually made with 50 to 60 percent of the full fuel load.

While the Blackbird is thundering off the Beale runway, a KC-135Q is airborne on its assigned course. A great deal of fuel is consumed during afterburner takeoff and climbout, and a quick refueling is essential. If the SR-71 crew can't immediately spot the tanker, the 135 will let out a squirt of fuel (which immediately vaporizes and looks a bit like a smoke trail) to aid visibility.

As the sky rumbles with Blackbird thunder, residents of nearby Marysville know another mission to an unknown destination is on its way.

Spouting twin tails of flame, there is no other shape in the sky like the SR-71. The landing gear has a retraction limit speed of 300 knots, so quick action is needed from the pilot as the Blackbird rapidly rockets skyward.

Once airborne, the Blackbird pilot's top priority is to find the tanker.

Most Blackbird pilots agree that the hardest part of flying the aircraft is joining up with the tanker. During training, if a student has repeated difficulties in connecting with the tanker's flying boom he is usually "washed out."

Against the deep blue California sky, the silhouette of the Blackbird is seen heading for its tanker rendezvous.

The SR-71A stabilizes its flight path and begins to move toward the flying boom protruding from the rear fuselage of the KC-135Q. Mating with the tanker is one of the most arduous tasks in Blackbird operations.

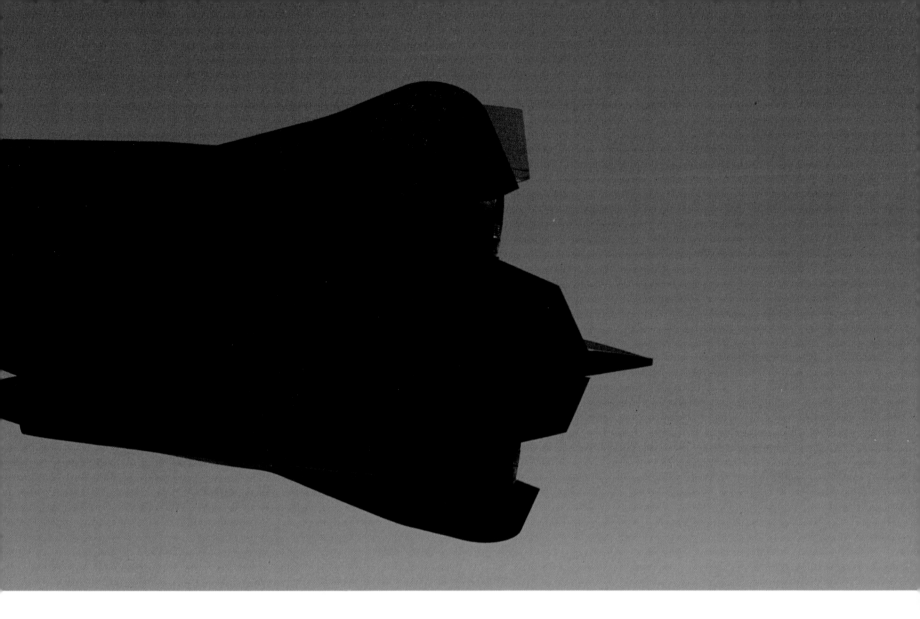

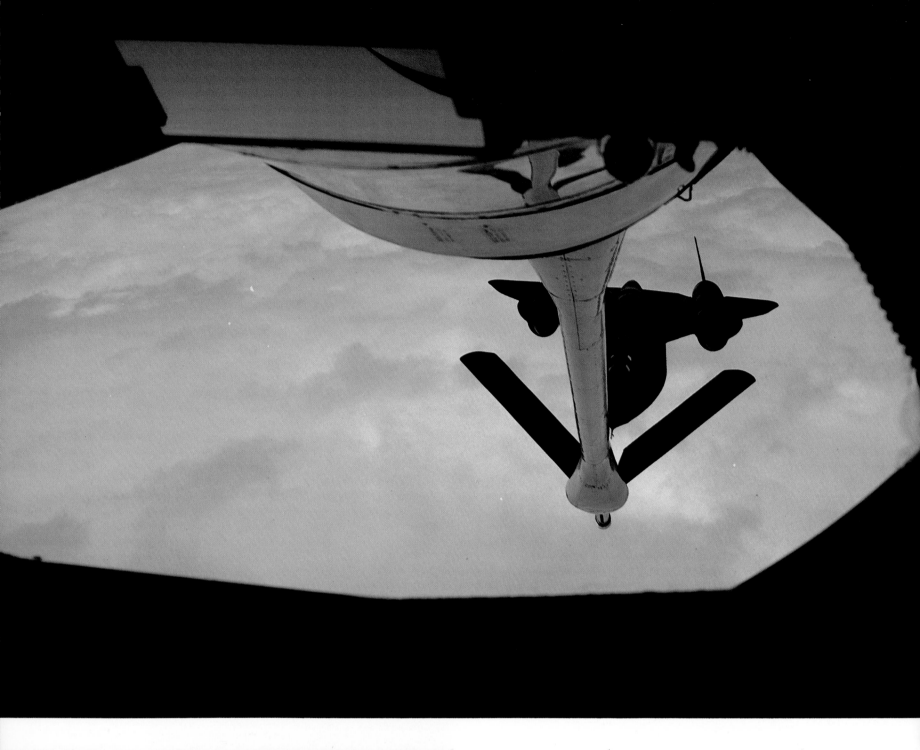

The fueling recepticle is located behind the crew position on the SR-71, making contact even that much more difficult. SR operations require a heavy commitment from the refueling fleet (30 KC-135Qs are assigned to Beale). In 1971, on a demonstration of extended supersonic flight, an SR-71 flown by Major Thomas Estes flew 15,000 miles in 10.5 hours. Even with frequent aerial refuelings, the aircraft was able to average an amazing 1,500 mph.

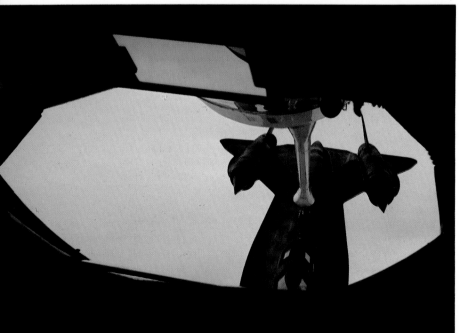

Contact! The SR begins to greedily take on JP-7 at a rate of 5,500 pounds per minute. Dozens of small leaks cause the fuel to stream from the SR's surfaces during refueling but once the aircraft reaches its cruising altitude and speed, the heated surfaces close up and the Blackbird becomes "leak free."

The Blackbird pilot concentrates on holding a precise formation during refueling. This view shows the RSO's small windows to advantage.

The KC-135Q is not an easy aircraft to "hand" fly so much of the refueling mission is done on autopilot. Here the pilot and copilot of a Silver Sow (SR crew nickname for the 135) prepare to receive their hungry visitor.

Connected KC-135Q and SR-71A as seen from a chase plane. Note the nose-up, drag-inducing attitude of the SR during the refueling phase.

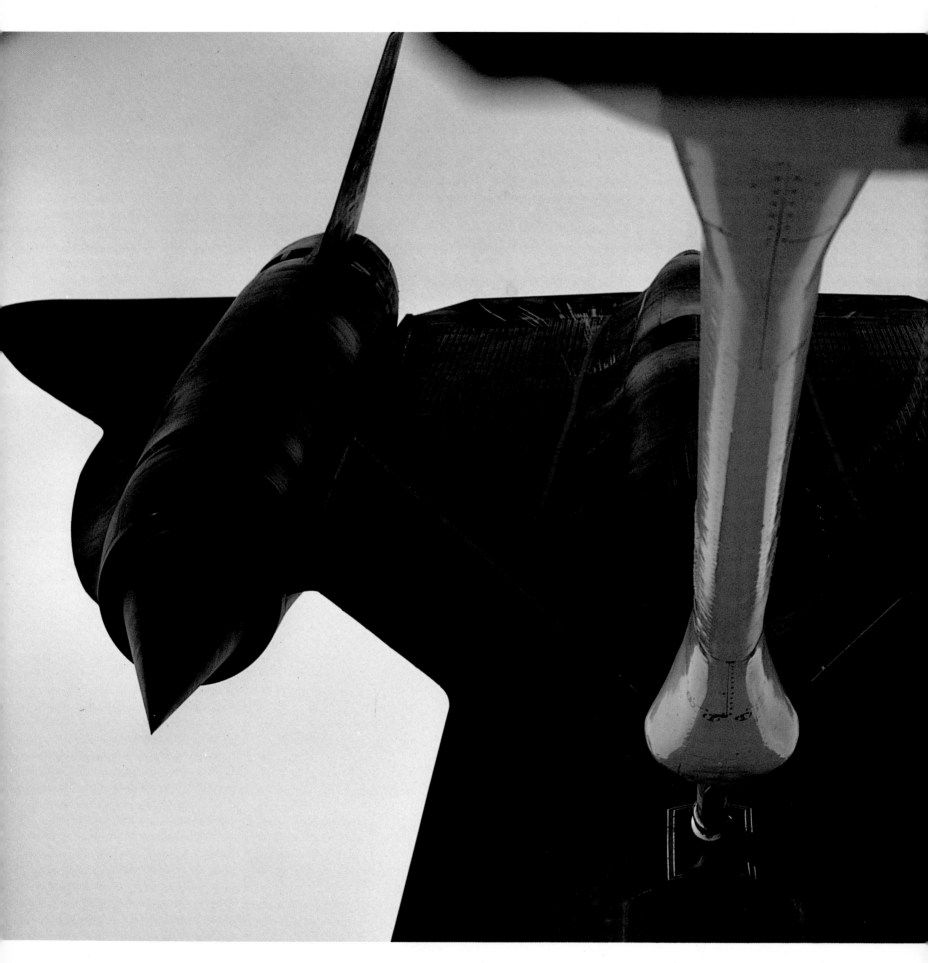

The boom is disconnected and SR-71A drops away after refueling. Note the vortices swirling from the chines on the outer edges of the engine nacelles and the fact that the upper surface is now wet with JP-7.

Boomer's eye view of the SR-71A (or "sled" as the tanker crews call the SR) as the flying boom is inserted into the refueling recepticle behind the crew stations. Note the many small JP-7 fuel leaks streaming from the upper wing surface—these will close up as the Blackbird accelerates and heads for high altitudes.

Power coming up, the SR clears the KC-135Q in preparation for its rapid climb to operational altitude. Note the chalked-on Jolly Roger insignia on the vertical tail.

The SR-71 is the world's first operational reconnaissance aircraft to be able to fly above 80,000 feet and the first to fly at speeds over Mach 3. Flying hours are carefully monitored on each operational aircraft and the planes are "rotated" between operations, maintenance and storage in an attempt to ensure a fairly even number of hours on the airframes.

Next page
A staggering 93 percent of the SR-71's airframe is constructed of titanium. This exotic metal has the advantage of being handily resistant to the extreme temperature of high speed flight, but it also has a distinct disadvantage: Titanium is very hard to work. Vendors supplying titanium SR parts for Lockheed literally reached the hair-pulling stage until more efficient methods of machining the difficult metal could be devised. Lockheed's Skunk Works also did a great deal of their own titanium fabrication—going on to produce more than 13 million parts!

Down and dirty, an SR-71A has returned from its mission to the edge of the atmosphere and is set up for recovery—in this case at US Air Force Plant 42, Palmdale, California. Some of the area's famous dry lakes (one of which is used for returning Space Shuttle landings) can be seen in the background. Touchdown speed for the Blackbird is about 155 knots.

Touchdown and mission successfully completed, the Blackbird's 40-foot-diameter braking parachute helps to slow the aircraft's tremendous forward momentum. During rollout, the SR is joined by a Mobile Control vehicle containing another SR crew who had been monitoring the aircraft's flight through its entire mission.

The crew chief carefully guides the Blackbird back into its "barn" after the completion of a flight. Once in place, technicians place fans next to the tires so that the brakes can cool. The SR's tires are specially made by BF Goodrich and impregnated with aluminum powder to help withstand the heat generated by the airframe during high speed flight.

*During its operational life time, the SR-71 has traversed
virtually every part of the globe. Today, however, with
improved diplomatic conditions between once hostile
countries and the great improvement in high-speed,
high-altitude missiles, each mission is carefully
considered before being launched. In 1981, a
considerable amount of international publicity was
generated when North Korea attempted to knock down
an SR with a barrage of surface-to-air missiles.*

84

In a current global political environment where it is more acceptable to use satellites or covert agents to gather intelligence on the activities of possibly hostile nations, the SR-71 still performs a very important role by being on call to go anywhere, anytime.

86

Waiting in its barn, a 9th SRW Blackbird stands at the ready for its next mission to the edge of space.

Chapter three

Dragons over Beale

To the casual observer, the shapes in the air over the northern California countryside could be elegant eagles, their wings spread far with the joy of the wind—lazily riding the thermals generated by the sun-warmed land. To those of a more pessimistic turn of mind, the dark shapes could be brooding vultures in search of a meal.

On almost any given day, the Dragon Ladies of Beale AFB are in the pattern, performing touch-and-goes, undertaking training flights or returning from ten-hour missions. The black shapes of U-2Rs and TR-1As have become commonplace to the locals living near the sprawling base. So common, they rarely look up to one of the huge shapes overhead.

The U-2R and TR-1A are probably the last of the long line of aircraft begun with the original U-2 prototype in 1955. Although just a bit outside the scope of this volume, let's take a brief look at the genesis of the U-2—the aircraft that would cause so much political embarrassment for the United States while contributing a great deal to our understanding of the Soviet Union and its Allies.

The idea for an efficient spyplane that could overfly the Soviet Union and avoid its myriad squadrons of interceptors was born in the early 1950s as the Cold War became a very unpleasant fact of life. During this period, the USAF operated a large fleet of intelligence gathering aircraft—most converted bombers such as the RB-29, RB-50, RB-36 and RB-47. All these aircraft were capable of gathering varieties of useful data but the four-engine piston aircraft were vulnerable to fighter attack, especially in light of increasing Soviet para-

noia regarding their airspace and just how far this space extended beyond their geographical limits.

The RB-36 could cruise above the MiG-15's top ceiling in relative safety but the Soviets were quickly developing new fighters to go after the camera-laden ten-engine aerial behemoth. When the Soviets exploded their first nuclear device during August 1953, the American military was completely taken by surprise. It was evident that the Soviets had recovered from the horrific losses suffered during World War II and that the Communist government was well on its way to seeing that such losses would not be incurred again. To find out more about what was going on inside the Soviet Union, the USAF built up its aerial intelligence gathering capabilities to include five Strategic Reconnaissance Wings by the mid-1950s. The Soviets were not passive while all this snooping was going on. When they could, they would attack and destroy American aircraft. Feeble excuses were made by the government as to why American aircraft and airmen were being lost near or over Soviet airspace. It became obvious that more capable, specialized aircraft were needed for the dangerous task.

A secret program code-named *Bald Eagle* was begun in 1953 to study the feasibility of building an aircraft that could operate over 70,000 ft. A range of at least 3,000 miles was also needed to give the aircraft the ability to overfly important areas of the Soviet Union and then recover at a friendly base. Martin, Bell and Fairchild were asked to provide proposals for a *Bald Eagle* aircraft. Each company came up with a different solution but an interim aircraft was the Martin RB-57D, another modified bomber but one whose wings had been stretched to an incredible 106 ft span for clawing up into the stratosphere.

Twenty B-57s were modified into the spyplane configuration under the program name of *Black Knight*. There were many structural problems with these aircraft and it was obvious that a specially built machine was required.

After a complete day of training flights for new pilots, the 5th SRTS's sole U-2RT dual-control trainer is seen on final to Beale AFB against a setting sun. Activated on 1 July 1986, the 5th Strategic Reconnaissance Training Squadron is the only training center for the TR-1 program. The unit operates two TR-1B and one U-2RT aircraft.

During this time, all aircraft companies were looking for extra work, and even though they had not been invited to participate, Lockheed Aircraft Company had come up with its own idea: an F-104 fuselage, modified and mated to a gigantic set of high aspect ratio wings.

Lockheed's fabled designer Kelly Johnson met with the head of the Central Intelligence Agency (Allen Dulles) and began promoting Lockheed's viewpoint on a spy aircraft. By this time, the modified F-104 concept had been dropped in favor of an all-new aircraft. The CIA needed a new means of gathering information on the Russians and Johnson cleverly played up this need by offering to deliver twenty spyplanes for $22,000,000 and within an astounding eight months. It was an offer the CIA could not refuse.

Lockheed Model CL-282 was a highly classified project (code named *Aquatone*) and assigned to Kelly's "Skunk Works," a small group of highly skilled personnel who had developed a reputation for getting the job done quickly and quietly.

The USAF originally dubbed the project Dulles' Folly but it soon became apparent to even the most dubious insider that the project was probably going to work. Metal on the prototype was cut in January 1955 and by August of that year, the prototype was ready to fly.

The aircraft had been given the designation U-2, meaning that the type was utility design number two—a vague terminology that Lockheed and the CIA hoped would not attract interest.

Groom Lake in Nevada was chosen as the test site for the new aircraft. The area was remote and the facilities were primitive—only a hangar and a few small buildings were erected.

The disassembled aircraft was flown to the test location by an Air Force transport and made ready for test hops by late July. The unpainted prototype was identified only by "001" on its tail when Lockheed test pilot Tony LeVier began taxi tests.

LeVier was taken by surprise as the aircraft lifted off at just 70 knots airspeed. The lightly loaded machine wanted to fly! The only way LeVier could get the plane to land was by literally stalling the

Highlighted by the lights from its hangar, a TR-1A awaits a nighttime flight. During the 1970s, NATO and Warsaw Pact countries had built up substantial ground forces, with the Soviet forces having greater numbers of weapons and troops. In order to carefully monitor these resources, a modified U-2R was proposed and the TR-1 was born. Thus, the rather negative (in a public relations sense) U-2 designation was finally dropped and the more acceptable Tactical Reconnaissance (TR) designation came into being, although the differences between the aircraft were minimal.

aircraft in the air—blowing out the main tires in the process. There was obviously lots to learn about this new bird!

More test flights quickly took place; the CIA's need for the aircraft was urgent. By the end of 1955, four U-2s were at the site and flights were extending upward to 70,000 ft. It was not an entirely risk-free process. The pilots soon came to learn that the U-2 was a difficult beast to fly. Even though the plane looked a bit like a streamlined powered glider, it had a mind of its own and several crashes occured during the training program. The CIA had picked a group of USAF fighter pilots to become the first full-time spyplane pilots.

Powered by a modified J57 engine operating on JP-7 fuel, early variants of the U-2 could almost reach 80,000 ft. Both Lockheed and the CIA were very happy with their new mount, the Soviets would have a hard time getting this aircraft!

During all this aeronautical activity, the CIA had other ways to get information on the Soviets. One of the stranger projects involved the massive Berlin Tunnel, which extended well into East Berlin, to eavesdrop on military conversations between East Berlin and Moscow.

When Allen Dulles visited President Dwight Eisenhower to report on CIA activities, he began his conversation with, "I've come to tell you about two acquisition projects, one very high and one very low."

Although a military man with an excellent reputation, Eisenhower was very worried when he learned about the CIA's new high (and low) altitude projects. In no uncertain terms, he indicated to Dulles that he wanted regular reports on the new aircraft and other CIA projects that could increase international tensions. Eisenhower had come up with a plan called Open Skies which would allow intelligence gathering aircraft to freely overfly other countries. He felt that this would help relieve international tensions by providing up-to-date information. The flights would be announced and closely monitored. The President had high hopes that Nikita Khrushchev would find this an agreeable solution to a vexing problem. During July 1955, Eisenhower went to Geneva, Switzerland, to meet with Khrushchev, but when the discussions finally got

An all-black TR-1A is seen with the training variant TR-1B. The early U-2s were not easy aircraft to master and the USAF had two TR-1B dual-control trainers in the TR order so that new pilots could be quickly indoctrinated to the type. The second cockpit, with full instrumentation, is installed in the Q-bay (short for equipment bay) immediately behind the original pilot position.

around to Open Skies, Khrushchev protested that the plan was a "bald espionage plot."

With the death of the Open Skies program, the U-2 became even more important. And there were several factions battling for control of the aircraft. Tough, cigar-chomping Curtis LeMay, commander of the Strategic Air Command (SAC, the operator of the vast majority of intelligence gathering flights near or over the Soviets), wanted the U-2 for his own. Referring to the CIA, LeMay stated, "We'll let those SOB's get in and then we'll take it away from them!"

An advisor of Allen Dulles told him, "Don't let LeMay get his fingers on the U-2."

In order to stop a feud between the CIA and SAC, the government agreed to let SAC recruit and train spyplane pilots while the CIA would conduct the missions. SAC officers began to visit the desert strip and view operations, learning from the pilots who had already flown the aircraft. "If I can't operate the aircraft, I ought to have a lot to do with training the crews," is a statement attributed to LeMay. SAC had gotten its foot in the door and was not about to let go.

U-2 overflights of the Soviet Union began in 1956. The Soviets knew they were being overflown from the start but they did not have a way of destroying the high-flying aircraft. The newest fighters could not zoom-climb high enough to get a shot at the aircraft. Early surface-to-air missiles (SAMs) did not have the range or reliability to hit the U-2s.

The CIA originally reasoned that the U-2 program would be good for only about three years, after that time they felt the Soviets would have developed a way of hitting the planes. Also, the U-2s were fairly fragile aircraft and the CIA thought they might become "used up" through operations or airframe fatigue. Little did anyone realize that of the approximately fifty-three U-2s built, most would be modified many times over and several would operate well into the 1980s.

The Soviets constantly complained through official circles of the overflights but the complaints also caused the Soviet military acute embarrassment since this was an admission of their failure to destroy the high flyers.

Each flight was carefully planned and launched from operating locations (OLs) in friendly countries such as Turkey—where a corner of Incirlik Air Base was converted into a U-2 OL. Security was more than tight and personnel were restricted to dumpy trailers on base. Francis Gary Powers recalled the setting as "grim" but the flying as "fun" and the pay "great." Pilot pay was around $35,000 which, in late 1950s currency, wasn't too bad—Powers purchased a Mercedes sedan, something most USAF lieutenants couldn't even dream of doing.

Eisenhower was very worried about the U-2 program and demanded that the CIA notify him before each flight so that he could give his personal approval or denial. Other operations with the U-2 were starting from Japan, Germany and Britain, but the plane remained hidden behind an incredible cloak of security. A Japanese magazine published photos of a U-2 that crash-landed in the open but the world press did not pick up on the fact that the U-2 was a very specialized aircraft. Perhaps Kelly Johnson had been right about the utility designation.

Life at the OLs was not a bowl of cherries. The pilots did not trust their CIA employers. Most felt that the ejection seats on the aircraft had been rigged with explosives to destroy pilot and aircraft if an ejection was attempted. The CIA also issued poison needles hidden in coins for the pilots to utilize in case they were forced down over the Soviet Union. They were not ordered to use the needles but there was a certain implication that the pilot should not survive a shoot down or flame out.

Once the CIA found out about the pilots' worries over the ejection seats, they volunteered to let the pilots inspect the seats. Distrust continued, however, and the pilots became more and more skeptical of the "Company's" attitude toward them.

Operations over the Soviet Union were not undertaken with a cavalier attitude. The missions were infrequent and carefully planned, the three-year knock-down estimate made by the CIA was in the back of everyone's mind. Yet, the information being relayed from the U-2s to the American intelligence community was invaluable. Long-range defense plans were being influenced by what the cameras and sensors aboard the U-2s were seeing.

It all came to an end on May Day 1960, when Francis Gary Powers was knocked out of the Soviet sky.

To this day, a great deal of confusion—real or fabricated—exists as to how Powers' U-2 (variously identified as USAF 56-6693, CIA Article 361, or NASA 360) was shot down. Powers recalled "a yellow-orange glow to the rear of the aircraft" before it fell out of control, beginning to come apart as the plane plummeted toward earth. Heading down over Sverdlovsk, Powers had his doubts about the ejection system and elected to manually extract himself from the aircraft. The plane became more uncontrollable as it began tearing itself apart through

TR-1B serial number 80-1065 is seen doing touch-and-goes during a training flight at Beale. The two TR-1Bs were delivered to Beale during 1983. Since this photograph was taken, both trainers have received the more traditional overall black paint scheme. The TR-1Bs do not carry the wing-mounted super pods.

97

a series of G-inducing maneuvers, and Powers was momentarily trapped in his harness and environmental fittings before being able to manually free the canopy and get out of the plane.

There has been various speculation that Powers' aircraft suffered a massive engine failure or was the victim of a "shotgun scatter" of SA-2 SAMs. The Russians had obviously grown tired (as well as being embarrassed) of the continuing overflights and were able to predict the American flight plan with a fair degree of accuracy. It appears most likely that Powers was downed by a concerted barrage of SAMs, but this is speculation and will probably not be verified for years to come.

With the downing of Powers, US spy efforts were thrown into the world spotlight and were received none too favorably. U-2 operations were cut back and Soviet Union overflights suspended. The CIA knew that one of their aircraft would eventually be lost but the actuality of the event struck them hard. Powers was put on public trial in the Soviet Union and the worldwide publicity was especially damaging to the United States. The amount of data on what was going on inside the Soviet Union dropped by ninety percent. Powers was sentenced to jail but, after two years, was traded for Soviet spy Rudolf Abel—a trade which was definitely in the favor of the Russians.

The Powers incident did not spell an end to U-2 operations; the missions took a different form. Overflights of Cuba proved that the Russians were building up a missile force on that island nation, resulting in another international incident.

By 1962, most of the U-2 flights had been taken over by the USAF—dropping many of the CIA operations completely. In other areas, the CIA continued to operate the U-2 unopposed.

In Taiwan, the CIA and the Nationalist Chinese conducted overflights of China which produced valuable information but also resulted in a number of U-2s being lost to enemy action. One of these lost U-2s may soon fly again; at press time negotiations have begun between an American aircraft collector and the Peoples Republic of China for the sale of the least damaged of these airframes and the wreckage of several others. The collector plans to restore the U-2C to flying condition and fly it on the airshow circuit.

U-2s continued to operate in many parts of the world on vital intelligence gathering missions but the number of aircraft was constantly decreasing

An all-black TR-1B is prepared for a training flight from Beale. Occasionally, TR-1Bs fly to RAF Alconbury, home of the 17th Reconnaissance Wing—the unit that operates the TR-1As in Britain.

Pilot in place, a U-2R prepares to depart its hangar at Beale for a training flight. The U-2R was put into production in order to supply the CIA and USAF with an intelligence gathering aircraft that would be superior to the rapidly dwindling numbers of "first-generation" U-2s. The first all-new U-2R made its maiden flight on 28 August 1967 from Edwards AFB with Bill Park at the controls.

100

due to accidents and operational losses. At this point, there is no way to tell how many of these losses were due to enemy fighters or SAMs.

By 1965, the USAF and CIA realized that the U-2 was still vital to the defense program but that airframes had dwindled making the program not viable. Kelly Johnson, Ben Rich and Fred Cavanaugh developed a new version of the aircraft, the U-2R, to satisfy the need for more U-2s.

The new aircraft was developed in much the same manner as the first U-2. The Skunk Works kept security very tight and of the first twelve production aircraft, six went to the USAF and six went to the CIA. The exact number of U-2Rs constructed is not known but is thought to be between one and two dozen. Some of these planes have been lost in operational incidents. One damaged U-2R was rebuilt into a dual-control U-2RT trainer and is based at Beale.

The first U-2R was flown by Lockheed test pilot Bill Park on 28 August 1967, and the aircraft quickly went into production. The cockpit was about forty-five percent larger, meaning that pilots could wear the more comfortable Dave Clark pressure suits and have more room in which to operate. Using the same J75-P-13B powerplant, the U-2R could utilize the engine's full 17,000 pounds of thrust since the earlier models had been thrust limited to minimize fatigue to their less sturdy airframes.

USAF pilot Paul Roberts prepares for a TR-1A flight from Beale during December 1988.

The U-2R is larger than previous U-2s. The wingspan increased from 80 to 103 ft, allowing an increase in payload. The fuselage is about one-third larger than earlier U-2s, allowing for the carriage of increased camera and sensor packages along with new countermeasures systems. The U-2R can carry almost 3,000 gallons of fuel internally in the wing, compared to the earlier model's ability to lift 1,320 gallons internally. The U-2R also incorporated many new advances in aerodynamics that had taken place since the early 1950s. Its fuselage is more aerodynamically streamlined, resulting in greater efficiency. The outer portions of the wings are capable of being manually folded, thus allowing the aircraft entry into narrow hangars.

When the first U-2 went aloft, it carried the civil registration N803X—signifying its assignment to the CIA. The U-2R test program was somewhat abbreviated so that the first aircraft off the line could be dispersed to Taiwan for Chinese overflights and to Bien Hoa, Vietnam, to gather information on the North Vietnamese.

Two U-2Rs flew nonstop to Taiwan where they had small Nationalist Chinese insignias painted on their airframes, and began operating over Communist China. This program operated quite successfully from 1968 to 1974 when the US government forged closer ties with the mainland government.

USAF U-2Rs were used to gain post-strike intelligence in Vietnam and gather communications intelligence (COMINT) from enemy radio signals. During these operations, at least two U-2Rs were destroyed, thus greatly reducing the USAF's already small fleet. With the fall of South Vietnam, U-2Rs continued operations from Thailand until finally being withdrawn from that nation in 1976 and sent on to other projects.

One of the most interesting projects involving a U-2R was the operation of a CIA aircraft off the USS *America* during November 1969. Highly classified at the time, results of the tests were later released. Lockheed test pilot Bill Park undertook the flights to demonstrate the U-2R's ability to operate from an aircraft carrier. Park had been an Air Force fighter pilot with no previous carrier experience so he went to Pensacola for carrier training in a T-2B Buckeye trainer. The catapult shots from the carrier were quite an experience to the skilled test pilot. "I'd never seen anything like a cat-shot in my life," Park later remembered.

Crew chief and mechanics swarm around a TR-1A prior to a flight from Beale. The sun shade helps keep the pilot cool while seated in the cockpit before takeoff. Even though he is plugged into the aircraft's environmental systems, the direct heat from the sun can make life a bit uncomfortable inside the Dave Clark pressure suit.

Tests showed that there was little problem bringing the U-2R aboard the *America*, a tail hook had been added to the rear fuselage and this became a fairly standard modification for other U-2Rs. The folding outer wing panels allowed the U-2R to be positioned on the carrier's elevators for trips down below to the hangar bay. "The U-2R demonstrated good waveoff characteristics and I felt at the time that landings could be made without a hook. We required very little special handling," recalled Park.

The US Navy was also showing interest in the U-2R as a platform for detecting enemy submarine activities from high altitude and great distances. Two CIA U-2Rs were assigned to the Navy in 1973 to test the advanced equipment needed for such operations. Initially operating from the CIA's North Base at Edwards AFB, a number of test missions were flown up and down the California coast with at least one of the U-2Rs wearing US Navy markings. The program proved to be successful but was not continued. At one time, Lockheed even made a study for the Navy on fitting the U-2R with a Condor anti-shipping missile. If this program had been carried through, the U-2R would have been the first variant of the type to be armed.

In 1976, the USAF decided to consolidate its U-2 and SR-71 operations at Beale AFB—which allowed for a more efficient marshalling of activities by the two types of intelligence gatherers.

With just a few original "short wing" U-2s still operational and a small number of U-2Rs in the inventory, the USAF was looking for supplemental aircraft. At this time it was thought that remotely piloted vehicles (RPVs) would take the place of manned intelligence gatherers. Boeing, Ryan and several other companies developed advanced concepts and prototype RPVs, but the aircraft suffered from early teething problems. Lockheed had proposed an RPV variant of the U-2R, and as interest in the RPV program (later to be called unmanned aerial vehicles, UAVs, and achieving a great deal of success when using much smaller airframes and sensor packages) waned within the USAF, Lockheed was in an ideal position to promote a new variant of the U-2R: the TR-1A.

Fortunately, the tooling and jigs for the U-2R production line had been carefully stored away rather than scrapped. A U-2R was pulled from operations and converted to a test bed for the new aircraft. The TR-1A designation stood for Tactical Reconnaissance and both Lockheed and the mili-

The stark but sleek lines of U-2R serial number 68-10338 are seen during a January 1989 test flight from USAF Plant 42 in Palmdale.

tary were glad to get rid of the U-2 stigma. Kelly Johnson recalls that General David Jones stated, "We have to get the U-2 name off that plane. We'll call it the TR-1."

As usual with these types of aircraft, contract negotiations were carried on in secrecy but the USAF and Lockheed announced on 16 November 1979 that a contract had been awarded to put the plane into production. Once again, Plant 42 at Palmdale, California, was chosen as the assembly site for the TR-1A and tooling was removed from long-term storage at Norton AFB.

The original contract called for the production of thirty-five aircraft including two dual-control TR-1Bs and two NASA ER-2s. The first ER-2 was flown on 11 May 1981 and effectively became the prototype for the series (since the first actual TR-1A did not fly until 1 August of the same year). Lockheed and the USAF actually put some fanfare into the production of the new aircraft by inviting the press to the initial rollouts.

Looking a great deal like the U-2R, the TR-1 was immediately identifiable by the giant "super pods" carried on the wings. The pods allowed for the carriage of more sensors, ideal for the plane's mission as a battlefield reconnaissance platform. The TR-1A carried the Hughes Advanced Synthetic Aperture Radar System that allowed a "look" into enemy territory at distances over fifty miles. The intelligence gathered by the aircraft could give NATO battlefield commanders immediate knowledge on enemy movements.

The TR-1As were optimized for the Precision Emitter Location Strike System (PLSS) mission which involved several orbiting TR-1As to gather and correlate transmissions and emissions from enemy equipment, and provide precise target information for attack aircraft or ground forces. However, the complexity of this program and the threat to the TR-1As from enemy aircraft eventually caused the PLSS role to be shelved.

In order to optimize the TR-1A's NATO mission, the 17th Reconnaissance Wing and 95th Reconnaissance Squadron were formed during late 1981. RAF Alconbury was chosen as the site for the new unit, and the first TR-1A arrived at the British base on 12 February 1983. The USAF eventually hopes to have as many as eighteen TR-1As stationed at Alconbury but budget constraints may reduce this number. Original funding for thirty-five aircraft has apparently been reduced to twenty-four aircraft, and when the second ER-2 rolls out of the Palmdale hangar during mid-1989, TR-1A produc-

Palmdale is also the center for U-2R/TR-1 repair, overhaul and modification.

106

tion will come to an end and the tooling will once again be stored. However, the U-2 series has a habit of coming back so it would not be wise to say that any portion of the TR-1A program is completely over.

TR-1As are regularly flown between Beale and Alconbury in flights that can take up to fourteen hours, giving an idea of the plane's awesome range. In the European environment, the TR-1A has proven particularly useful in gathering electronic intelligence. Photographic packages can also be fitted and, like the U-2R, several different types of noses can be fitted to the TR-1A to accommodate different sensor packages. The huge super pods can also be differently configured depending upon the particular mission.

The 17th RW's Dragon Ladies have become a common sight in the English countryside as the all-black TR-1As head out on missions or practice flights. Pilots used to the generally sunny climate of Beale have to quickly accommodate themselves to the British climate, especially in relationship to the TR-1A's handling qualities on rain-slick runways. TR-1B dual-control trainers make regular visits to Alconbury to check out pilots and conduct training flights while airframes are shuttled back and forth to Palmdale for overhaul or further modifications.

Whatever the future may hold for continued TR-1A (or derivatives) production, it is assured that the type will have a long life with the USAF, operating well into the next century on a variety of missions important to national defense.

The U-2R and TR-1A are basically the same aircraft with minor equipment and wiring differences. Most TR-1As mount super pods on the wing but this is not a sure-fire identification feature since some U-2Rs have super pods and some TR-1As don't! The exact number of U-2Rs built is not known.

Lockheed TR-1A specifications

Span	103 ft
Wing area	1,000 sq ft
Aspect ratio	10.6:1
Length	62 ft 9 in
Height	16 ft
Empty weight	15,500 lbs
Maximum weight	41,300 lbs
Sensor weight	3,000 lbs
Fuel load	1,175 gallons/ 7,650 lbs
Maximum speed	373 kts @ 70,000 ft
Limiting mach number	0.8
Ceiling	80,000 ft
Maximum range	6,300 miles
Rate of climb	5,000 fpm (initial)
Load design	−1.5/+3G
Climb to 65,000 ft	approx 35 min
Takeoff run	650 ft
Landing run	2,500 ft
Engine	Pratt & Whitney J75-P-13B of 17,000 lb static thrust

TR-1A and U-2R are ideal for intelligence gathering over countries that do not have sophisticated aerial defense systems. For example, during a suspected Soviet build-up of advanced MiG fighters in Nicaragua, intelligence material was gathered that made the Free World community more sympathetic to the Reagan Administration's claims against the Sandanista government. U-2Rs have been operated in the markings of Nationalist China and there has been speculation in the press that the aircraft has been flown by pilots of Allied nations including Great Britain and the Federal Republic of Germany.

After the completion of a successful mission, a TR-1A pilot and crew chief go over the logs prior to putting the aircraft back in its hangar. Note the condensation on the upper wing caused by a reaction of the JP-7 fuel.

Previous page
The glider-like shape of the fuselage of the TR-1A is particularly evident in this head-on view of an aircraft taxiing out at Beale in the early morning fog. Visibility from any of the U-2 series is not particularly good due to the amount of equipment in the cockpit, the restricted nature of the pressure suit's helmet, and the large sunshade that is part of the canopy. A small rearview mirror provides a limited view of what's going on to the rear of the aircraft.

Poised for a dawn takeoff from Palmdale, this view of a TR-1A shows the aircraft's black "iron ball" paint finish to advantage. Rough to the touch, the paint has small specks of iron imbedded in the pigment, helping confuse hostile radar systems and giving the plane a certain "stealth" quality.

Chapter four

White birds by the bay

Naval Air Station Moffett Field is situated in the middle of a massive urban land-sprawl that crowds around San Jose, California. The field is immediately identifiable by three giant hangars which dominate the horizon. These hangars were built to contain the massive silver sky behemoths that the Navy operated during the last gasp of the airship program that had begun before the start of World War I. The huge airships were used by the Fleet as scouting and patrol platforms. Some were equipped to carry their own squadron of protective fighters, which were lowered from hangars built into the airship's hull and then launched and recovered using a complex trapeze device. These giant vessels of the air are now, unfortunately, just memories recorded on fading photographs.

The base, named after one of the pioneering Navy airship officers, is now the West Coast home to the Navy's Lockheed P-3 Orion subhunters and patrol craft. The air is constantly alive with the rumble of big Allison turboprops as P-3s launch for training flights or operational deployments. Moffett is a very busy Naval Air Station.

Another famous Lockheed product also calls Moffett home, but these aircraft are not assigned to the US Navy. On the northwest section of the sprawling base is the NASA (National Aeronautics and Space Administration) Ames facility. Casual visitors to the facility may at first think they have wandered onto a college campus by mistake, by the look of the buildings. The many buildings at Ames house a variety of NASA offices responsible for conducting far-ranging experiments. Many of these programs are jointly conducted with national and international universities and, over the years, have contributed greatly to man's understanding of the air, space and earth.

Much as the Navy's portion of the base is dominated by vintage airship hangars, NASA Ames is dominated by its backdrop, the world's largest wind tunnel—so large that complete aircraft can be inserted for aerodynamic testing.

Ames is also home to a variety of aircraft. The interested observer can spot such diverse flying machines as an AV-8B Harrier, the massive C-141 Galaxy airborne observatory and (the focus here) a fleet of beautifully maintained Lockheed U-2/ER-2 aircraft—for NASA Ames is also home of NASA's High Altitude Missions Branch.

The upper atmosphere is of great concern to NASA—especially since large "holes" in the earth's protective ozone layer have been discovered. Before NASA obtained U-2s, and later ER-2s, much of the high-altitude experiments were undertaken by three Martin/General Dynamics RB-57Fs operating from NASA Ellington in Texas. With the phase-in of the U-2C, the RB-57F (a temperamental and difficult-to-maintain aircraft) was gradually phased out of high-altitude flying. And the addition of the much more mission capable ER-2 basically put an end to RB-57F operations. "The ER-2 is a tremendously capable aircraft whose airframe is easily adaptable to many different upper atmosphere tests and experiments," stated Ron Williams, a Lockheed pilot under contract to NASA to fly the U-2C and ER-2.

NASA's association with the Lockheed high-flyers goes back a long way. When Francis Gary Powers was shot down over the Soviet Union on May Day 1960, a cover story was quickly fabricated by minions within the Dwight Eisenhower Administration that the U-2 flight was an operation being conducted by NASA and that the pilot had "blacked out" during high-altitude experiments, the plane accidently drifting into Soviet airspace. Unfortunately, the NASA administrator at the time was persuaded to foist this story upon the international press and was later made to look a fool when Nikita Khrushchev announced the pilot was alive and talk-

Jerry Hoyt points the nose of the U-2C directly at the camera. The U-2C is distinguished by the large avionics hump atop the fuselage. Virtually every first-generation U-2 has been rebuilt and modified over and over to correspond with assigned mission profiles.

ing. President Eisenhower had been assured by the CIA that a pilot would not survive an "accident" over the Soviet Union. "We have remnants of the plane, and we also have the pilot, who is quite alive and kicking!" boasted a victorious Khrushchev who was making the most of a rare opportunity to bask in the favorable opinion of world press. NASA spokesman Walter Bonney's statement that the U-2 was on a NASA "weather research flight" was internationally debunked.

The damaging and dangerous incident of the first U-2 shoot-down highlighted the aircraft's unique capabilities and the fact that NASA *would* like to have a U-2 for legitimate upper atmosphere experiments. It would not be until April 1971, however, when two veterans of CIA and USAF programs were transferred to NASA Ames. Both aircraft had lengthy past histories of a variety of covert operations. (In fact, the log book of one aircraft contains several signatures of Francis Gary Powers as he signed off the appropriate forms following Soviet Union overflights, making the log a very historic document.) But NASA wished to sever these past ties and had the planes stripped of their rather sinister black paint. An attractive white, gray and blue paint scheme was applied along with the titling "Earth Survey Aircraft" along the planes' spines.

The two U-2Cs were the seventh and eighth U-2s in the initial production lot for the CIA and both planes had been modified many times over the years in response to different mission requirements. The planes were also given civil registrations, N708NA (USAF serial number 56-6681) and N709NA (USAF serial number 56–6682). The military serial number was also painted on the airframes so that NASA could take advantage of certain Federal fuel tax benefits.

These two U-2Cs had last seen military service with the Strategic Air Command's 4080th Strategic Reconnaissance Wing and had participated in the vital overflights of Cuba during the Missile Crisis. At one time during their operational life with the CIA, both planes had been converted to U-2G configuration (which meant that the planes were equipped with tail hooks and other associated systems to

Ready for a mission. Jerry Hoyt stands by Lockheed U-2C 709, which carries NASA's distinctive new logo on the vertical tail. The vintage U-2C, which was retired from operational duties in the first quarter of 1989, was specially flown by NASA for the aerial photographs in this book. Hoyt is wearing the early MC-3 pressure suit and holding the suit's portable air conditioning unit. Each suit had to be custom-fitted since space inside the cockpit of first-generation U-2s was at an absolute minimum.

Carefully dressed against possible harmful effects of nitrogen, a NASA crewman replenishes the U-2's systems prior to flight.

Sun shade in place, the pilot of U-2C 709 goes through final cockpit and route checks prior to launching from the NASA Ames facility at Naval Air Station Alameda. NASA shares the Moffett runways with the Lockheed P-3 Orions of the Navy's West Coast patrol wing headquarters. The pods under the wings of the U-2C were installed to collect examples of cosmic dust at high altitude.

enable the planes to be operated from aircraft carriers). During 1964, carrier compatability trials were undertaken aboard the USS *Enterprise.* "Old 709 is even more unusual," said one of the NASA pilots, "in the fact that it was equipped for carrier operations as well as being modified for aerial refueling—the only U-2 to be so modified."

The U-2, with its standard tremendous range, must have taxed even the most dedicated of pilots who had to sit in the cramped cockpit for additional hours. The exact nature of the U-2G missions has not been made public but it is presumed that the aircraft were so modified to be recovered aboard carriers when friendly landing sites, after long over-flights were not available.

The veteran U-2Cs became common sights as they steeply climbed away from NASA Ames on a wide variety of missions that encompassed everything from capturing cosmic particles in the upper atmosphere to detailed mapping of the earth's resources to recording natural disasters and their effect on the environment. Massive amounts of data were accumulated on almost every function around the globe, delighting the scientists with the detailed results.

The majority of NASA high-altitude flying is undertaken by pilots working for Lockheed and contracted to NASA, with two NASA pilots assigned to the High Altitude Missions Branch. Most of the maintenance and modification to the aircraft is also undertaken by Lockheed employees under contract. The high percentage of Lockheed employees in the program adds an evident *esprit de corps* and the group works in very close conjunction with NASA to create an efficient, mission-ready force.

Perhaps the biggest boost to the NASA High Altitude Missions Branch was the arrival of the first ER-2 (Earth Resources 2) at Ames on 10 June 1981. Effectively being the prototype for the TR-1A series for the USAF, the NASA plane was delivered in "house" colors and registered N706NA (USAF serial number 80-1063). The plane was flown to Ames from the Palmdale, California, assembly point by Martin Knutson. The ER-2 had made its maiden flight on 11 May 1981, with Art Peterson (a Lockheed test pilot) at the controls, and flew its first NASA mission on 12 June 1981. NASA's second ER-2 was delivered to Ames during April 1989.

"Lots better," is how Ron Williams describes the handling characteristics of the ER-2 when compared to NASA's earlier U-2Cs.

Taxiing past an impressive array of NASA facilities, 709 heads to the active runway for its five-and-a-half-hour particle sampling flight.

AIRCRAFT FLIGHT REPORT
AND
MAINTENANCE RECORD

349

Every flight of NASA's U-2/ER-1 fleet is carefully logged; engine and airframe hours are closely monitored. At the time of this photo flight with 709, the vintage intelligence gatherer had accumulated over 7,000 hours of flying time.

"That's right," said Jerry Hoyt. "It is a much more mission capable aircraft. The ER can haul a bigger load of equipment while going higher and further with more reliability." Both pilots, however, agreed that the ER-2 was almost as hard to fly, with some quirky characteristics just like the U-2C.

The last U-2C (NASA 709) was retired from NASA service in April 1989, and was flown from Ames to Palmdale where it was painted in an overall black scheme and then ferried to Warner Robbins AFB in Georgia where it was put on display as part of the base's heritage program. The other U-2C, which had been withdrawn from service sometime before, is now on display in front of the NASA Ames gift shop.

Before the final flight of NASA 709, an exciting decision was made to go after seventeen world altitude records with the vintage aircraft. Plans were quickly drawn up with the National Aeronautic Association (the organization that administers record flights), and the U-2C was flown to Edwards AFB, where it was prepared for the two-day event. On 17 and 18 April, pilots Jerry Hoyt and Ron Williams blasted aloft to meet and beat all the records, placing the U-2C firmly in the record books. Two days later, the aircraft was retired for painting and its final flight to Georgia.

"In a way, we were sorry to see the old 'short wings' go," said Williams, "but the ER-2s are much better suited to the NASA mission."

NASA has also obtained a TR-1A, N708NA (USAF serial number 80-1069), that was surplus to USAF requirements. At the time of our photographs, the TR-1A was being operated without its distinctive "super pods," while NASA's first ER-2 was having its super pods fitted with a variety of exotic instrumentation for a mission to Norway in order to continue research on the ozone layer.

The ER-2 mission to Norway is an example of just how important the aircraft is to NASA's continuing search to discover more about the planet on which we live. In January 1989, the ER-2 was dispatched from Ames in company with a NASA Douglas DC-8. The former airliner had been heavily modified by NASA, its passenger interior stripped and instruments packed into the space. The flying laboratory made fourteen flights for the ozone experiment, with thirty scientists, representing ten scientific teams, gathering valuable information on the ozone problem. The DC-8 flew along the lower edges of the stratosphere while the ER-2 went to its normal operating altitude, trying to remain within 250 miles of land during each mission profile—the gliding distance of the ER-2 from altitude in the event of an engine failure. "That part of the world really has a hostile environment," stated one pilot.

"If you were forced to eject and not quickly found, chances of survival would be minimal."

The cost of the scientific expedition was estimated at between $8 million and $10 million, a fairly minimal amount when considering the effects that a depleted ozone layer could have on the earth. Small reductions in the ozone over the Arctic region "could be more serious because most of the people reside in the Northern Hemisphere," stated Estelle Condon, manager of the Airborne Arctic Stratospheric Expedition.

"Operating on the edge of space," said John Arvesen, chief of operations for the NASA ER-2, "allows us to gather vital material and conduct important experiments that would be otherwise almost impossible without the ER-2."

Not all NASA ER-2 programs are as dramatic as the ozone experiments, but many are equally important. NASA "short wings" and "long wings" (nicknames for the U-2C and ER-2/TR-1) have traversed the globe on projects vital to our understanding of ecology. The destruction of the Brazilian rain forest and its far-reaching effects have been carefully mapped. The explosion of Mount St. Helens was documented by camera-toting NASA birds while the incredible amount of pollution thrown into the atmosphere was also plotted. "It was really something to fly over that mountain while it was exploding," said Ron Williams whose aircraft's cameras captured very dramatic images.

Even though the "short wings" are part of history, NASA is ably supplied for its varied duties with the newer aircraft. "Much more pleasant to fly," said Jerry Hoyt. Hoyt and Williams both had extensive

This MA-2 helmet was original late 1950s U-2 equipment. Tight, uncomfortable and with a tendency to fog up, the helmet is now just a souvenir of a NASA pilot.

Suited up and ready to go, a NASA pilot takes the short ride in the PSD van to the Ames flight line and the waiting aircraft.

Assisted from the NASA High Altitude Missions Branch PSD van, technicians will aid the pilot in getting in the aircraft and attaching seat and parachute harnesses as well as plugging the suit into the aircraft's environmental system. This pilot is wearing the newer S1010B full pressure suit which can only be worn in the second-generation intelligence gatherers (U-2R/TR-1/ER-2).

USAF experience before joining NASA. Both also flew combat over Southeast Asia, Williams in the F-4 Phantom II, Hoyt in the F-105 Thunderchief. "I volunteered for the USAF's U-2 program after a tour in Southeast Asia," recalled Hoyt. "At that time you were given a pretty good battery of physical checks and you were tested out to see how you would fit in with the other squadron members before being accepted. It was important that an individual meshed well with the squadron.

"While in the USAF, I put in over a thousand hours flying U-2s and flew out of quite a few different operating locations. In the military, you were given an assignment, went out to your aircraft and flew the mission. Sometimes you did not know what the mission was about. What I like about NASA is the fact that we pilots are directly connected with the entire mission. We work with the scientists, help select the appropriate cameras and sensors for their experiments, and then are heavily involved in the debriefs; we are completely involved in the experiments from beginning to end and we get to see the final results. I personally feel this sort of contact is very satisfying."

NASA's Jim Barnes was retiring about the same time the U-2C was withdrawn from service. Barnes has over 6,000 hours in U-2s, a record that probably will never be broken. He was one of the original carefully selected pilots who flew the first top-secret aircraft at a classified desert base. Barnes was a fighter pilot and flew F-86 Sabres during the Korean War. "Hell, I tried to convince Kelly Johnson that he wanted bomber pilots to fly those things [U-2s]. Fighter pilots fly fairly short missions while the bomber guys are used to staying up and droning around for hours. Kelly said no because he wanted individuals that were used to operating by themselves."

Barnes made his first U-2 flight in August 1956. "It was a fairly informal affair," he recalled. "You were given a systems and cockpit checkout, got in and flew the thing after taxiing around to get a feel for the controls." From that point, Barnes has been intimately involved with the U-2, flying for NASA and other government agencies.

"With these type of aircraft," said Jerry Hoyt, "you get to see some things that other pilots never will. You get to see the sky divided into three parts: bright light on one side, sort of an afternoon directly overhead, and blackness on the other side. Quite often you're so busy in the cockpit that there isn't much time to look outside but we do get to see some very special sights."

NASA is developing new uses for its three-plane fleet and there is little doubt that the "white birds by the bay" will continue gaining international headlines as their experiments gather information to benefit mankind.

Wearing the bulky but more comfortable S1010B suit, the pilot carefully ascends the TR-1A's boarding ladder.

The instrument panel of the U-2C is surprisingly
spartan and gives a good idea of the aircraft's age.
Pencils stand at the ready for the pilot to make notes on
his knee pad during the particle gathering mission.

U-2C 709 in flight near California's Big Sur. Although painted in NASA colors, the aircraft still carries its original USAF serial number (56-6682) on the sides of the fuselage. Even though assigned a military serial number, it is thought that 709 spent a considerable portion of its working life with the CIA, then operating with the USAF before being handed over to NASA. NASA 709 has recorded flights over Russia, China and Cuba while under CIA control and was flown by Francis Gary Powers.

Lockheed U-2C specifications

Span	80 ft 2 in
Length	49 ft 8½ in
Wing area	600 sq ft
Aspect ratio	10.6:1
Wing loading	40 lbs/sq ft
Height	15 ft 4 in
Empty weight	13,900 lbs
Maximum weight	24,000 lbs
Limiting mach number	0.8
Maximum speed	240 kts @ 65,000 ft
Ceiling	72,000 ft
Maximum range	4,500 miles
Climb to 65,000 ft	approx 40 min
Engine	Pratt & Whitney J75-P13B of 17,000 lb static thrust

The last flying U-2C is shown here in formation with its much newer stablemate, the TR-1A, on a beautiful December 1988 day over California's scenic coastline. The U-2C is piloted by Jerry Hoyt; the TR-1A is under the command of Ron Williams. The TR-1A is some 40 percent larger than the U-2C, can carry a heavier payload higher and farther, and is a bit easier to fly.

Looking a bit like an old science fiction film's character, Jerry Hoyt displays the MC-3 high-altitude suit and portable air conditioning unit. After the retirement of the last U-2C, this outfit became an immediate museum piece!

With its underwing particle sampling pods in place, the U-2C basks in the setting sun at NASA Ames—one of the huge dirigible hangars rising in the background. Once housing a single member of the Navy's mighty airship fleet, the all-wood structures (registered historic landmarks) now easily gobble up many P-3 Orion subhunters from the units based at Moffett.

A setting sun casts a few final glints of light off the broad wings of the final flying U-2C. The aircraft has been assigned as a gate guardian for Warner-Robbins AFB in Georgia, to be painted black as a remembrance of flights more hostile than those undertaken by NASA.

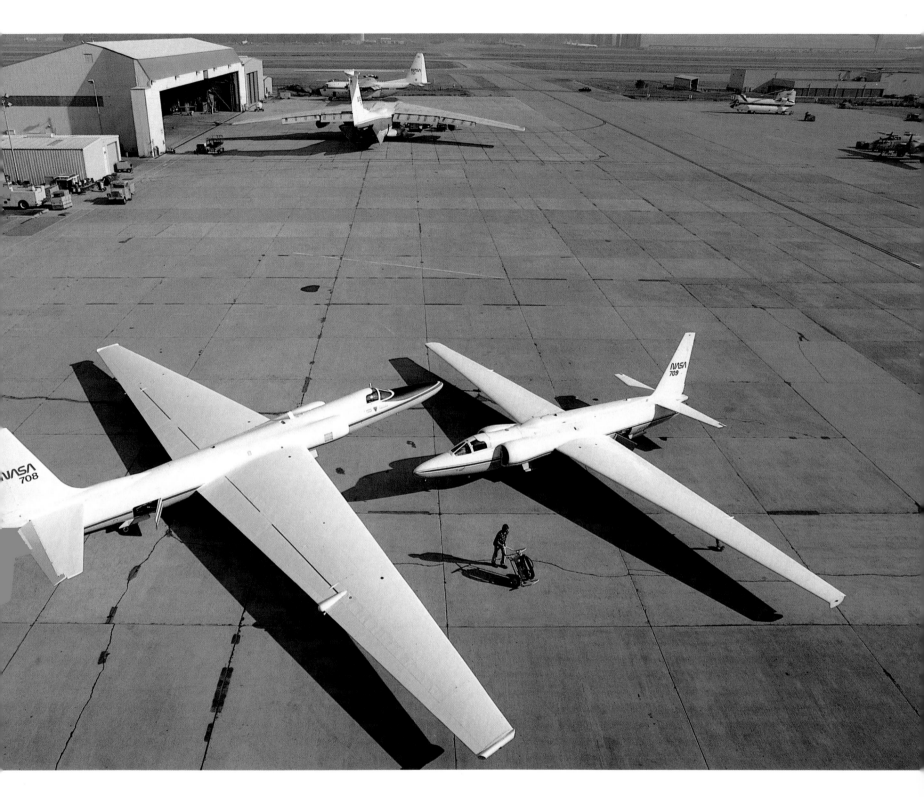

Taken from a precarious perch atop one of the giant NASA Ames hangars, this photograph illustrates the vast differences in size between U-2C 709 and TR-1A 708. The TR-1A, serial number 80-1069, last served with the 17th Reconnaissance Wing at Royal Air Force Alconbury, England, before being declared temporarily surplus to USAF needs and transferred to NASA. Easier to fly and more mission capable than the first-generation U-2s, the TR-1 is definitely the "Cadillac" of the U-2 family.

Lockheed and NASA technicians perform pre-flight maintenance on the TR-1A. The aircraft's single main landing gear leg and its dual wheels are shown to advantage.

NASA operated ER-2 706 (USAF serial number 80-1063) which was, effectively, the prototype of the TR-1 series. The ER stands for Earth Resources. The ER-2 is basically a TR-1 minus some of the military equipment and systems wiring. Here the ER-2 is seen undergoing maintenance and modification in the NASA High Altitude Missions Branch hangar prior to a January 1989 flight to Norway. Note how the nose section swings open. The ER-2 and TR-1 can accommodate several different nose sections depending on the mission. The TR-1A in the background does not carry the wing-mounted super pods.

137

Tight formation. Any member of the U-2 family of aircraft is difficult to fly in formation because of the type's unique handling qualities, but Ron Williams makes it look easy as he displays the TR-1A's massive 103 foot wingspan. Kelly Johnson designed the original U-2 to be, basically, a powered glider that could achieve great heights and distances through lightweight construction and aerodynamic cleanliness.

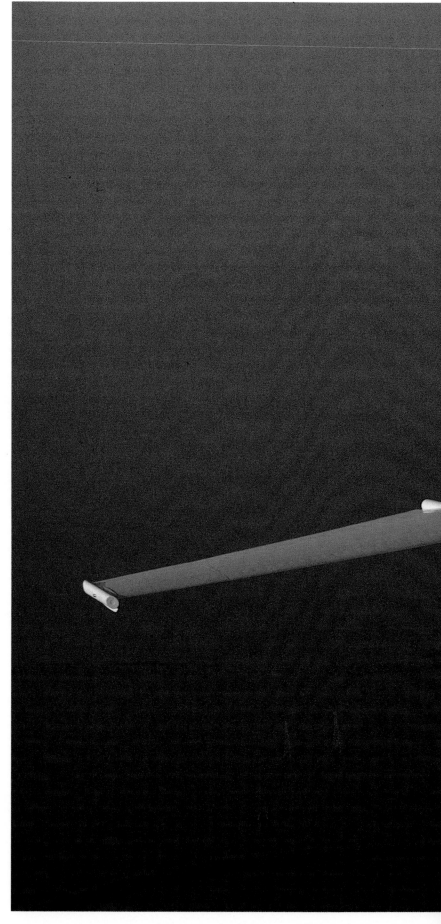

Q-Bays behind and below the pilot's position carry the major portion of intelligence gathering equipment when the TR-1A or ER-2 is not equipped with wing-mounted super pods. The elongated nose area can also carry a wide variety of sensors and cameras.

NASA White Bird pilots usually avoid banks of more than 15 degrees in order to keep the aircraft within their fairly narrow G-limits and to avoid handling problems. In this view, the TR-1A and U-2C are seen skirting San Francisco's famous marina (the vintage US Army Air Corps Crissey Field—now, unfortunately, just a parking lot, can be seen to the right).

Few American cities are more photogenic from the air than San Francisco and its magnificent bay. The White Bird flight heads out over an atypical fog bank with the beautiful Golden Gate Bridge making a dramatic background.

*Passing over a striated cloud deck, the two NASA White
Birds provide a look at the past and future of Earth
Resources aircraft. The new TR-1As and ER-2s will be
able to gather larger quantities of information relating to
the earth and its environment, and the information will
be channeled into methods of keeping the earth's
environment "friendly" to mankind.*

*We're not quite sure what commuters on the Golden
Gate thought about the very unusual sight of a NASA
TR-1A and U-2C passing overhead, but the historic
formation was recorded passing across the world-
famous bridge and into rural Marin County, with the
high-rise city of San Francisco as an attractive
backdrop.*

In the hands of a skilled photo/intelligence interpreter, information gathered by the NASA White Bird fleet will be of immediate use to the global community.